MW00415622

"When life is sweet, say thank you and celebrate.
When life is bitter, say thank you and grow."
—unknown

PRAISE FOR Sigrid Olsen

"Sigrid Olsen is that rare person who lives a life of creativity and entrepreneurship in seeming perfect harmony. Her memoir about her own path of art, reinvention and overcoming adversity is a gift to us all."

Dana Buchman
Fashion Designer
Author: A Special Education

"At first, infatuated with her clothes, then smitten with her retreats... and finally... impressed with a true appreciation and respect for the warm, talented and giving woman herself... I am happy to know Sigrid as a friend and fellow creative. Sigrid's journey of re-invention is one that speaks to her optimism, perseverance and strength. Her story as a designer and renaissance woman is bound to inspire countless others on their paths to wellbeing and fulfillment."

Kathy Davis
Creative Visionary Officer
Kathy Davis Studios

"Sigrid Olsen is my hero. She has dealt with physical and professional challenges with courage and resilience by healing in deeply personal ways that we can all learn from and be inspired by."

Kim Johnson Gross
Author: What to Wear for the rest of Your Life
Co-Author: Chic Simple Book Series

"Sigrid Olsen is an extraordinary artist and an extraordinary human being, who embodies balance in all its aspects. I look forward to learning from her remarkable life."

Sarah Green
Film Producer

"With candor and beauty, Sigrid Olsen creates this inspirational portrait of all that life can be, when challenges and change are met with courage, creativity, and a belief in our own inherent strength of spirit. Sigrid Olsen writes as beautifully as she paints!"

Rev. Bonnie Draeger, MS, MDiv
Executive Director: Friends & Cancer
Author: When Cancer Strikes a Friend

What's a creatively compulsive designer to do when her life is turned upside down?

After multiple major upheavals that left her gasping for air, Sigrid did what any burned-out, former-hippie, fashion executive would do...she packed up a bikini and some art supplies and went to the beach. On the eastern shore of Tulum, Mexico she reconnected with a long dormant yoga practice and lost herself in meditation until the layers of stress peeled away and she could breathe again.

Photo Credit: Andrea Hillebrand

SIGRID OLSEN
MY LIFE Redesigned

Embracing Change, Aging Gracefully and
Finding Magic in the Simple Things

by
Sigrid Olsen

First Electronic Edition: January 2018

First Print Edition: April 2018

Print book and eBook design & formatting by D. D. Scott's LetLoveGlow Author Services

Cover Photo Credit: Tory Williams Photography

For my family,
who taught me how to give and receive love.

For my love, who always believes in me.

For my friends and creative collaborators.
You know who you are.

And especially for all the women
who have taken the leap of faith
to join me on retreat.

Thank you. You inspire me.

The New York Times

FASHION & STYLE

Her Forced Retirement

By ERIC WILSON   AUG. 13, 2008

GLOUCESTER, Mass.

THE call came late at night on the first Monday of January, delivering the news that Sigrid Olsen had feared for six months. Liz Claiborne Inc., after a review of its brands, was dismantling her 24-year-old fashion business, closing its 54 stores and laying off dozens of employees, including the designer herself.

Ms. Olsen, who spends much of the year at her longtime home here, began to call her staff in New York to explain what was happening in advance of a corporate announcement that would be made the next day. But what she could not explain was what had led to the demise of a peppy brand with a passionate customer base and peak sales of about $100 million, or why the sputtering Liz Claiborne conglomerate, which had entertained offers for Ms. Olsen's label and others, had not chosen just to sell it.

"I thought that we were one of the brands they would want to keep and nurture," Ms. Olsen said. "That was more shocking than anything."

Foreword

It was a photograph and the newspaper headline in the New York Times that first caught my eye: Such an attractive woman. 'Forced into Retirement'? I read on. Sigrid Olsen. I knew that name! I owned her clothes, but to be honest, I thought she was a corporate figment—like Betty Crocker. Or Aunt Jemima. What a delightful surprise! There really is a Sigrid Olsen.

According to the article, Liz Claiborne, Inc was closing 54 Sigrid Olsen stores nationwide.

It went on to say, "Her tale is in many ways emblematic of how those customers are being pushed aside for a younger (in a business that defines the 'older woman' as over 35!), trendier and more lucrative shopper."

Sigrid's story really resonated with me... how she was "turning a difficult situation into a positive experience." Though we'd never met, I thought we were kindred spirits. I got a phone number. In case she answered the phone, I printed out some prepared 'talking points'. I was nervous. I waited for her to call me.

I was in the car when my cell phone rang. I recognized the area code. Disregarding my own common sense, I answered the phone—but only long enough to ask if I could call her right back, which I did in less than ten minutes. Picture me on a summer day, sitting on the grassy island of a parking lot in the shade of a small tree. We talked for about twenty minutes and connected on so many levels. For one thing:

She said she was sitting under a tree too.

Later we met in person and, though the headline writer missed the point—Sigrid had not been 'forced into retirement', she was 'forced into 'reinvention''—the New York Times was absolutely right on another point: Sigrid Olsen was certainly a vibrant 55-year-old!

Since then Sigrid and I have had many thought provoking and inspiring conversations. We have a lot in common, but the contrasts are significant too: I don't think she spends as much time as I do dithering over what to do or how to get something going. Sigrid is a custom blend of right brain and left-brain: Inspiration wrapped in common sense. A doer with a sunny disposition, she has overcome so many obstacles and keeps on moving ahead. Her story is one that will inspire, especially for women of our generation who realize that, with less think and more do, life can hold the promise of getting better and better with age.

Jane Pauley
New York City
November 2017

Table of Contents

INTRODUCTION

"Even castles made of sand fall into the sea, eventually."
—Jimi Hendrix

I feel most at home on islands, surrounded by water. Watching the surf ebb and flow is a meditation—the rhythm, the repetition, the soothing fizz of the water's edge as it meets the sand. It reminds me that life is also a series of waves. Sometimes they roll in smoothly, as predictable swells that lift me up gently. Other times, they are raging torrents that turn me upside down, gasping for air.

Ironically, it's those breathless, potentially ruinous moments that provide the most valuable lessons. My heart has been broken open so many times, yet I'm happier than I ever have been. Even when the trials are painful or shocking, and my first instinct is to plunge into despair, I find my way to see it as a gift. Negative emotions give way to a fierce impulse to learn from it and **thrive**.

My faith has been tested over and over. After three major upheavals: breast cancer, the demise of my company and the loss of my spouse, I was faced with the life-changing question:

How do you reinvent yourself when you thought your life was all figured out?

My journey to this answer is at the heart of these pages. Writing this book, I revisited my past through the myriad journals and sketchbooks I've kept throughout my life. Opening each one, I was struck by the alchemy of words and pictures; how they reveal my innermost thoughts and feelings so accurately.

While my circumstances have changed over the years, my inner self remains the same. I am an ambitious overachiever with a hankering for spiritual enlightenment. As a compulsively creative person, I struggle daily with the conflict between my innate tendency towards productivity, and my soulful desire for serenity. As much as I try to control everything, I know life will unfold beautifully, if I just stay out of the way.

Most people recognize my name from the fashion label I launched years ago. My career, which has spanned over three decades, is still a huge part of who I am and how I define myself. Yet now, it is integrated into a lifestyle that embraces the profound life lessons that have propelled me to where I am today. Ultimately, I am grateful for the catastrophes that took me out of my comfort zone and gave me the impetus to redesign my life.

The fashion business took me on a wild ride, one where I was catapulted into the stratosphere, and my feet didn't touch the ground for a long while. I went from being a hippie entrepreneur, who rode a bicycle to my first business meeting, to a corporate executive with a huge staff, a hectic schedule and a multitude of product lines that ranged from women's clothing, handbags, jewelry, scarves and eyewear to bedding and bath accessories. My ad campaigns were seen on the pages of *Vogue*, *Elle* and many other fashion magazines. It was a thrilling experience, exhilarating, and full of opportunity, but exhausting beyond belief.

Creativity was a valued attribute in my family of origin, so it was perfectly natural for me to aspire to make my living as an artist. But I never expected to become a fashion designer. I entered that world through an unusual path. A passion for textiles and printmaking led me to experiment with potato printing on fabric. I built a repertoire of iconic print motifs—seabirds, leaves, flowers, fish and geometric patterns—that spoke to my love of nature and indigenous cultures. My first clothing collections were based on these whimsical prints and my unique, sun-drenched color palette.

My success was a result of pure passion, incessant hard work and tremendous good fortune. Early on, I met some very astute and well-connected people, who helped launch my career in the early eighties. It didn't take long for our small start-up to become a major fashion player in the industry. At the peak of our business, the line was carried in most major department stores (Bloomingdales, Nordstrom, Dillard's, Parisian, Marshall Field's, Burdine's and Macy's to name a few), as well as thousands of small specialty boutiques and, eventually, fifty-plus SIGRID OLSEN retail stores across America and Canada.

In 1999, our company was purchased by the Liz Claiborne Corporation. After the merger, I stayed on as Creative Director for my women's clothing label, and shuttled between offices in Wakefield, Massachusetts and Seventh Avenue in New York City. I led a talented team of designers and enjoyed the glow of success, while the line blossomed, growing exponentially over the next eight years.

I learned so much during my corporate years—not all of it good. I understood quickly that a public corporation worships at the altar of growth and profit. I learned to manage multiple agendas, while trying to retain the authenticity and integrity of my brand. I began to realize, as my leadership role grew in importance, my creative-self began to wither. As time went on, there was a gradual, almost imperceptible shift of power away from me, as the brand visionary, to the executive offices of the corporation.

Then, in January 2008, my world was turned upside down. Liz Claiborne Inc. announced the closing of SIGRID OLSEN as part of a corporate strategy to streamline their holdings during the economic downturn. In one swift corporate pronouncement, my business was over, and I found myself, for the first time in my adult life, without a job. I went from being a sought-after designer, with my hand in dozens of creative projects, to a woman with nothing to do, my life-long dream cut short.

End of story? No. In fact, the beauty of *MY LIFE Redesigned* is that it shows how the most profound revelations I've gained were a direct result of the biggest upsets of my life. After all my unexpected upheavals, I had to take a leap of faith to trust my intuition again. I had to let go of regret about the past and stop worrying about the future. I had to learn to believe in the present moment and put my energy into finding beauty and inspiration in the simple things.

Luckily, by nature, I'm an optimist. When faced with mayhem and drastic events, I've discovered the best way to endure change is to embrace it. I thought I was strong. But I had to be stronger. To conquer my feelings of loss, there was no way but through. So, after my side trip into the "real world," I turned to a spiritual practice that had lain dormant in me for 25 years. It was perfectly natural for me to be drawn back to the things that I knew would heal me—yoga, art and meditation—especially now that I had nothing but time on my hands.

Once I regained my equilibrium, I began to see how many of the same skills that served me as a designer would guide me on my personal reinvention: Determination. Passion. Gut-instinct. Honesty. Unflinching self-scrutiny. Creativity. Expansive thinking. I recognized the elements of my career that energized me and felt empowered to reject those that drained me.

One thing I knew right away: I missed the connectivity I felt with other women – my staff, my peers and especially my

~ 4 ~

customers. When the news of my company's demise was made public, I was literally deluged by letters, emails and phone calls. Encouraged by this outpouring of love and support, I was determined to create a new, more intimate community to express my authentic self and my renewed vision. That's what led me to initiate my art and yoga retreats, which I have hosted in beautiful places around the world, from Tuscany and Provence, to Tulum, Mexico and Ojai, California. They have given me a renewed sense of purpose and hope. My retreats have also provided a real-life window into the mind and heart of today's female…how she lives and what is really important to her.

Connecting with women, both personally and professionally, has led me to understand the depth of our collective longing for peace and serenity, and the intensity of our thirst for self-awareness. We all have dreams. And we make decisions that lead us either closer to, or, in some cases, farther away from manifesting what is in our hearts. Life is essentially a creative endeavor. It's a series of careful edits—the choices we make dictate the way our story will unfold. We keep tweaking until we get it right. (Spoiler alert: you never actually do, but that's OK.) The goal is to keep growing and learning, not to win a prize. It's a lifelong process.

Now, in my sixties, I finally know what I need to sustain me. I remind myself every day that *this is enough*—I am fortunate to have found a life that works for me, even if it doesn't always feel smooth or even abundant. Achieving this is no accident. I have consciously designed my new reality, not just by following my heart, but with clear intention, plenty of work, and heavy doses of faith. While my life is still a work-in-progress, I feel I have found my path.

So much good has materialized as a result of my self-discovery. I reclaimed my name and have revived my business on my own terms. I've cultivated new friendships, new love, and a life that nourishes me in so many ways. I'm grateful for the gift of perspective my struggles have brought me. That long-range vision helps me discern what matters and let go of what doesn't. I no longer have to please the world. Even though I have resumed the creative work I love, my career doesn't define me. I appreciate who I am and value every hard road I've traveled. Instead of dwelling on the pain, I have learned from it and moved on.

I created this book to be a place of refuge, a reminder of beauty and a source of inspiration...something to keep, to share with a sister, daughter, or friend. It's about my journey as a creative being and the subsequent soul-search that resulted in my designing a new life. Even though each of our personal narratives has its own unique arc, I believe the lessons are universal. Most of us share a desire to go deeper in life—to understand the undercurrents that move us emotionally and propel our life choices. We can create the life we want, redefine success, achieve serenity and choose happiness. My hope is that my story strikes a chord with you, and opens up your heart.

Namaste,
Sigrid Olsen
Sarasota, Florida
November 2017

Sunshine in the Garden

~ 8 ~

In the Beginning

"Teach your children well. Their father's hell will slowly go by.
And feed them on your dreams—
the one they picked, the one you'll know by.
Don't you ever ask them why. If they told you, you would cry.
So just look at them and sigh and know they love you."
—Graham Nash

Last winter, while I was lounging on the beach in Mexico, I caught sight of someone who conjured up a vivid memory of my mother, Lucia, who died several years ago. Looking up from the book I was reading, I saw a tanned, bikini-clad body and was immediately transported to childhood summers at the seaside, where I spent hours playing while my mother soaked up the sun. Now, here I was, happily baking on the shores of the Yucatan, as though channeling her spirit. I felt a lump rise in my throat—missing her, knowing how happy she'd be to know the life I've chosen revolves around the sea.

My heart expanded, recalling how she taught me to love this— the feel of the sun on my bare skin, the sound of breaking waves in the distance. Did she teach me, or did I simply absorb her passion for the ocean through the salty fluid in utero? Her love for the sea was deeply rooted in her sense of what life was all about. As is mine. Fondness for the wild ocean and the heat of the sun has become a key underpinning of my life's work. I paint the sea, sell beachwear and take people on pilgrimages to be inspired by the magic of the shoreline. Thanks, in part, to Lucia.

Water was only one of my mother's passions. Throughout her lifetime, well into her later years, Lucia had an obsession with two things: culture and the sea. The former was a focus of hers as she guided me through my adolescence, hoping to instill a European love of the humanities in an ordinary American teenager. I wasn't always very receptive. But her love of the ocean was something that I inherited fully without question and now I can't imagine living anywhere else.

Most of what I cherish in life has come to me through my family. All the doubts and misgivings my parents may have had about the choices they made and the disappointments we all endured were redeemed by one thing. **Love.** Children thrive when they know they are loved, even if their lives are less than perfect. All the baggage of expectations aside, every accomplishment I've made in life is a result of the loving support I received from my family while growing up.

I was blessed with a complicated and interesting childhood. It wasn't always easy or even happy, but in the scheme of things, it was a good one. Rural Connecticut in the mid-fifties was a wonderful hotbed of artists, writers and intellectuals, and my parents fit right in. Like so many who settled in the Litchfield, Roxbury, Washington area, my father, Van, and his aristocratic, Italian-born bride, Lucia, dove right in to the local scene. Having just moved from New York City, they were gratified to find such an interesting community, which included the sculptor Alexander Calder and author William Styron.

Art and culture permeated the refined world in which I was raised. Our home was a tasteful blending of Danish modern furniture and Italian antiques, with artful flourishes that my mother created with carefully chosen paintings, flowers and ethnic pottery. I learned to appreciate a wide range of music from Beethoven to Dizzy Gillespie, both of whom still remind me of my early years.

My lineage (Danish and Italian in particular) was, and still is, a powerful influence. I feel as though the blood in my veins carries with it a magic elixir of imagination, creativity and style derived from the two design-driven countries that produced my ancestors. I also believe that my European roots enable me to enjoy life's pleasures without guilt. I'm a real mélange of my heritages. The contrasting temperaments of this mix explain the dichotomy of my personality—emotional, sun loving, passionate and impatient from the Italian side—cool, calm, diligent and brave, courtesy of my Scandinavian roots.

My parents met in Naples, Italy during the war. Handsome naval officer meets beautiful, free-spirited daughter of a count. My grandfather's title—*Conte Gege Balsamo De Loreto*—actually meant very little, except that his eccentricities could proliferate unhindered by the constraints of having to make a living. Also, it made my mother *La Contessa*, a title that she grudgingly gave up when she became an American citizen, decades later. Fortunately, whenever she went back to Italy for her annual visit, they still referred to her as *La Contessa*, which of course she loved. She never lost her exotic accent, and she never really took to being American. In fact, years later during my adolescence, when friction arose between us, usually fueled by her melodramatic reaction to something I said or did, my complaints about her hysteria were always met with the same response:

"I can't help it. I am *Italian*."

When I was a young child, my mother was the most beautiful and inspiring woman to me. She was charming and passionate and loved me with a fervor I never understood until I had my own children. I flourished in the warmth of her affection and I longed for her love and comfort whenever I felt alone or uncèrtain. To me, she represented beauty and good taste, and I was always grateful that she took an interest in my thoughts and feelings. At six, I was a lonely little girl, and still unburdened by her fixation on loving me. I basked in it.

For Lucia, life turned out much differently than she expected. She was educated and socialized in the dreamy, pampered nest of the Italian upper class. She was wooed by the intellectuals of her time—writers, actors, musicians, artists, filmmakers—many of them communists and revolutionaries. Her young adult years were spent in animated conversation, smoking cigarettes and discussing philosophy with her friends in seaside cafes in the crazy mixed up Neapolitan metropolis that she loved with an irrational zeal. In her imagination, life would always be an endless stream of languorous days perched on rocks by the sea discussing politics and sipping wine.

No wonder she was disappointed.

Reality was nothing like that. Not only did she leave the idyllic seaside of her youth in Naples to emigrate to New York City when she married my father, but she lost touch with the intoxicating stimulation of her Italian intellectual friends when she became an American housewife. At first, they lived in Manhattan with my father's frenetically social-climbing parents, and I'm sure she enjoyed the excitement of the parties and events that peppered their days and nights. But then they made the (perhaps misguided) decision to move to the country and she soon found herself in very unfamiliar terrain in rural Connecticut. It was an empty existence for my mother, who thrived on sun and lively interaction. I imagine her alone in a small apartment with a new baby, looking out at the dreary grayness of a New England winter, feeling hopeless and alone. The despair she felt after abandoning her beloved home in Italy never really left her.

In Connecticut, my parents eventually gravitated toward a community of artists and intellectuals who helped ease the bleak emptiness my mother felt in the expansive wilderness. She also sought out other expats and enjoyed the fertile culture of a new group of intellectuals in the outskirts of New York City. They lived near Roxbury, Connecticut where they met a whole crowd of interesting people. It was almost as though there was an invisible yet palpable thread binding artists together even in the most random places. As a curious six-year-old, I absorbed by osmosis, the banter, the visual stimulation and the ambitions of this creative crowd. Looking back, it was an amazing time and the people with whom I came in contact had a subtle, yet lasting effect on me.

I witnessed first hand that it was possible to be both creative and successful.

My parents' circle of friends intrigued me. I recall going to "movie night" at the home of writer Bill Styron, being welcomed warmly by his wife Rose and even playing with their kids. The films were a bit beyond my grasp at the time, serious and subtitled, but I got the sense that writers, filmmakers, artists and those who mingled with them lived in a rarified world that was made richer by their worldly experiences. I could tell that this kind of stimulation was important to my parents, and even though I didn't quite understand much of the conversation, it would be important to me one day, too.

I was fascinated by the sculptor Alexander "Sandy" Calder and his wife Luisa who were also family friends and occasional dinner guests at our house. My mother showed me pictures of all the quirky things he made for his home. For instance, the kitchen lights he crafted out of used *Medaglio D'oro* coffee cans (the same brand of coffee we had at our house) seemed an incongruous connection with the gigantic mobiles and stabiles I had seen in museums in New York. All her life, my mother proudly wore a pin he designed for her, fashioning her initials LVS in hammered silver. (After her divorce, she continued to wear it, but upside down.) It still looks so fresh and contemporary, proof that great design never gets old.

When I was young, my parents owned a small, mid-century modern furniture and gift store that engaged each of their creative talents—my mother's eye as a buyer and my father's flair for charming customers. It was far ahead of its time with great Scandinavian teak pieces, sleek Dansk pottery, modern stainless steel flatware and eclectic gifts from various countries. In a town known for colonial antiques, this shop was an oddity, but it attracted a refined and artsy crowd.

It was there that I learned about window displays, visual merchandising and the importance of gift-wrapping. The last point was indelibly impressed on me one year when Calder presented my parents with a solution to a problem he observed during a Christmas rush, watching my mother struggle to gift wrap a package in the back room. He devised a handy gadget to assist her—a sculpted wooden "finger" that pivoted on a handmade lever to hold the ribbon as she tied her bows. The design of this little device captures perfectly his delightful nonchalance and love of whimsy. He was a natural creator without an ounce of self-importance. When asked by a reporter to describe the meaning of his artwork, he replied in his usual gruff manner, "I don't know. I just make the stuff."

From this unusual background, I emerged an enthusiastic, wide-eyed child with a conviction that art was indeed a viable and honorable livelihood.

By the time I was seven, my parents divorced. Maybe my mother had grown tired of my father's charming flakiness and was lured by the prospect of becoming the wife of a doctor, hoping that this would lead her to a new level of security and stature. Another decision she lived to regret.

My father remarried quickly as well, and a whole new chapter of my life began. He moved back to New York and went on to have two more children with his third wife Gilda. When I was twelve, I had the surprise of finding out that I had an older half-bother, Fred, whom my dad had fathered with his first wife, Amy, long before he met my mother. Dad and Fred never knew each other until one summer when Fred, an accomplished musician, came from his home state of Montana to New York to perform with the Montana Centennial Band at the 1965 World's Fair. My family expanded even more, and I was intrigued and happy. I was born an only child, and now, there were four of us.

Long stretches of my childhood were spent in New York with my father and his new family. I was thankful to have younger half-siblings because they gave me something to do during those long summer vacations spent away from my familiar life in Connecticut. I was always looking for activities to save me from the boredom that plagued me so much of the time. I gladly traded my only child status for the joy of being a big sister. At that age, my maternal instincts were untainted by the complications of adolescence. I was enchanted with baby Lisa when she was born, vowing to take care of her forever, after the birth of her younger brother Danny. Growing up an only child, I had no frame of reference for how parents could raise two kids, so I was afraid she would be neglected when she had to compete against a new baby. It turned out that I was able to love them both and she has remained an important part of my life especially after Danny's suicide twenty years ago. Our family has gone through painful hardships, deaths and disappointments, but we have managed to stay close and find laughter through it all.

My mother's remarriage turned out to be both good and bad for me. I gained a new stepfather, whom I accepted immediately, welcoming the attention of another adult in my life. But I also inherited a family of five stepsisters and brothers who weren't so crazy to have a new sister. I was like an eager puppy, cooped up alone for too long, so when I was introduced to this whole new cast of characters, I welcomed the experience with open arms, trying endlessly to engage my new step- siblings in games, longing to be part of their clan. I had no idea what kind of trauma the divorce had caused them, and it never occurred to me that they would resent me as collateral damage. We had moments of camaraderie, but for the most part, my overtures of friendship were largely ignored. There was one bright light in the murky relationship I had with this new family and that was Martha. She was the youngest of the five siblings, just a year behind me in school, and she actually liked me, though I know she was torn by divided loyalty. We shared a room until I was fourteen when she moved away permanently to live with her mother on Martha's Vineyard.

Today, I give thanks for this difficult experience for two reasons. One—it taught me to rely on my own company, to be self-sufficient and learn to read other people's reactions carefully, though I admit it's probably also the source of my weakness for people pleasing. Two—it introduced me to my stepsister, Martha. She is the only one of these siblings with whom I have stayed close all these years, and she turned out to be the perfect person to help me when I established my yoga and art-infused Inspiration Retreats. Forty years later, it seems our unlikely pairing had a purpose.

My stepfather Frank became my close comrade and mentor, helping me navigate much of the difficult terrain of my adolescence. As a teenager, my relationship with my mother became strained, and he was there to manage the fallout. I began to see myself as different from my mother, regarding her as a disappointed dreamer who had no right to tell me how to live my life. I saw her friends as intellectual snobs and her hopeless hedonism as unrealistic and spoiled. I was a sunny optimist born to an Italian Contessa prone to melancholy. Whether it was in reaction to her brooding or a simple gift of nature, I just wanted to be happy. I learned early on that this was my responsibility and I could not count on anyone else to do it for me. More than once, this balance of optimism and pragmatism provided the strength to propel me to success.

Now when I look back on my mother's life—her penchant for angst, her constant overanalyzing of everything and her unrelenting desire for something more than a "conventional life"— I understand it so much more clearly. I *get it* now. What she lacked most of all, what haunted her every day was this…she had *no sense of purpose*. She felt she had relinquished her own dreams by putting her faith in the men in her life, and to some degree, that was true. They disappointed her, causing a lifetime of regret about the many poor choices she made. She became almost too paralyzed to take action.

Her indecision was so pronounced she chose a vanity plate for her car that read "FORSE" which in Italian means "maybe." At least she had a sense of humor. The irony, however, is that the untrained American reads this as "force" and assumed she was stating her strength and power as a woman, which couldn't have been farther from the truth.

Once I was grown, she floundered, unable to grow up herself. She had funneled everything—her passion, adoration, hopes and fears—into me, her only child. Being loved like that was incredibly affirming, but it was also a burden. I knew I could never satisfy the empty spaces inside her, and I vowed I would never do that to my own children. When she moved to Santa Barbara, and I was entrenched in business and family on the East coast, she would call me and moan, "I'm so *depressed*. It's as though I don't even have a daughter. I have nothing to live for." High drama. Annoyed as I may have been with her whining, I understood that she needed something of her own to wake up for each day. We all do.

Maybe that's why I'm a bit obsessive about filling my days with meaningful activity. I have always sought profound purpose with a fervent determination. I was an existentialist by the eighth grade, inspired by reading Emerson and Thoreau in English class. The seed of self-sufficiency was planted then and nourished throughout my lifetime.

As an artist, I always have a sense of purpose. There's no limit to where my creativity can take me. I don't have to depend on anyone else to provide my motivation, therefore I am responsible for my own happiness.

From a very young age, I displayed a fixation and talent for art. As an only child, I spent hours with my markers and paints. It kept me occupied when nothing else could fill the void. My family recognized and encouraged this, maybe realizing that it was not just a balm for my loneliness, but an actual passion that could grow into something extraordinary someday.

My father brought me up to treasure art and the mess it brings. He bought immense packages of crayons, pencils and magic markers for my birthdays. He instructed me on how to care for my art supplies and scolded me for leaving my brushes standing in turpentine. He studiously critiqued each new drawing or painting and gave me very adult reviews of my work.

Like him, my creative expression has taken many forms over the years, reflecting different periods of my life, but there's a unifying quality to all of my work (even the fashion design) that conveys my optimism, as well as a love of color and repeated pattern. It was there at age five and is still strong today.

Through all decades of my career and despite my overwhelming dedication to fashion design, my father never abandoned his ambition for me to be an artist. His definition of that role was narrower than mine, and my success as a designer didn't satisfy it in the least.

One memory that illustrates this so perfectly is when he visited me at my showroom years later on Seventh Avenue in New York. Our plan to meet for lunch was a rare opportunity for us to get together since my demanding schedule left little time for fun. Our showroom space was beautiful—spanning the entire twenty-sixth floor—very modern and upscale. At the entrance, behind the reception desk, was an enormous light box, illuminating fashion images from our latest ad campaign, and my name in huge letters. It was a scene I had never imagined in all my years of drawing and painting, and I was excited to show it to my father, who, even though he lived less than a mile away, had never seen it.

When he arrived at the glass doors, I buzzed him in, feeling an odd mix of embarrassment and pride. Embarrassed by the extravagance and proud of...well, I guess the same. I gave him the full tour, walking through several rooms, past walls and walls of outfits hanging on stylish steel grids, past buyers and sales people working at chic metal tables. Since it was market week, there was a buzz of activity, a real-life spectacle of success. He followed me silently around this foreign territory until it was time to rush out to keep our lunch reservation.

As we waited, arm-in-arm, for the elevator, I asked: "So... what do you think?"

His response: "It's great honey, but when are you going to get back to your art?"

Well, fifteen years later, I got "back to my art", and I confess, he was delighted.

My mother was just as supportive of my artistic leanings, but much more impressed with my success in the fashion world. She was chic and stylish in her own way, and my father raved about the collection of clothes she had tailored for her in Italy for her voyage to America in 1952 to marry him.

While I strove to be nothing like my mother, I grew to appreciate and even cherish the essence of her. My father remained a steadfast supporter of my art with little, if any, comprehension of the ambition that led me to a career in fashion. Yet, his encouragement lifted me past any self-doubt that plagued me along the way.

When all the ambitious competition to *have* more, *do* more, achieve more is cleared away, what are we left with? People, family, beauty, good food, great conversation, laughter, art, nature, sunshine, wine—all the things I learned to love from my parents.

Here is what I have observed both as a daughter and as a mother—*parents teach us as much with their failings as with their successes*. I consider this to be my most valuable inheritance.

~ 22 ~

Early Influences

"Don't let the noise of other's opinions drown out your inner voice. And, most important, have the courage to follow your heart and intuition. They somehow know what you truly want to become. Everything else is secondary."

—Steve Jobs

I celebrated my seventh birthday sick in bed with strep throat and remained there nearly the entire summer of 1960. It was an odd time of transition for my mother and me, right after my parents' separation. I was vaguely aware of the changes that were happening—my father moving back to New York and my mother getting ready to marry someone else. She and I had moved in temporarily with a friend of hers and we were in a state of limbo while the summer elapsed. I hadn't quite grasped the full impact of what was really happening, and my fever made me feel as if everything was seen through a blurry cloud of delirium.

I finally rallied enough to celebrate my birthday at the lake with a few friends. Seeing a picture of me from this day makes me sad. The faded hues of the photo give it that bleak air of desperate emptiness that is typical of snapshots from the sixties. I'm a small, pale figure in a striped sun suit, perched with a pail and shovel on the edge of the beach. No one is playing with me, and I look at the camera with a weak attempt at a smile. It wasn't the best year of my life.

Transitions are hard for everyone. But somehow, as a child, I just went along with the flow as best I could. I remember feeling apprehensive when we moved to my new stepfather Frank's house in a nearby town that fall, just in time for second grade. I can imagine my mother's concern, putting me in this unfamiliar situation. It wasn't easy for either of us, but my sense is that it was much harder for her. The sickly summer had been so bad for me. This had to be better.

My mother had to adjust to the reality of becoming stepmother to five strangers, as well as having to care for the rambling, twelve-room colonial that Frank had bought to house his new expanded tribe. She had grown up with servants in Italy, was raised by a governess and had always lived in the city. This was a huge change. Having me was about all she could handle. I learned to cope. I'm not sure she ever did.

Frank's five kids were on a custody schedule where they moved back and forth between their mother and father every two weeks. Our big house was totally full during the intervals when they were with us, and then desolately vacant the other weeks of the month. To Frank's kids, my mother and I represented the upheaval of their lives and a deep resentment festered for years. For Lucia, their departure every two weeks was a relief. But for me, it left a huge void.

I felt more alone than I ever had as an only child. I can still remember the aching emptiness of the long, lonely afternoons, when I was the only one around. I would sit passively, watching the stark light of winter fade into dusk outside my window, waiting for time to pass. The house felt barren and way too quiet. The sense of lonely desolation is probably what triggered my existential quest. "Is this all there is?"

The cure for my despair was always productivity. If I could create, then life had a purpose. I worked hard to find things to keep me busy. I looked forward to tackling my schoolwork, and when it was done, I still had my art. My bedroom was a constant mess, with multiple projects in progress, and my mother was on a continuous campaign for me to straighten it. I immortalized this struggle in a Mother's Day card I made for her one year that had a pen and ink sketch of her standing outside the door to my room, which was etched with crisscross lines, representing the hopeless jumble that was its usual condition. Her mouth is fixed in a scream, one hand on her hip, the other holding a cigarette (she was smoking in every picture I ever drew of her from my childhood years). The word bubble above her says "Dio mio!" She laughed when I gave it to her. It was our thing, this ongoing argument.

My childhood games also foretold my entrepreneurial future. My activities usually had some creative yet organizational element—stuffed animal hospital with shoebox beds and well-kept medical charts, plastic horses with elaborate wooden block corrals and colorful yarn bridles, library books with handmade index cards to classify them. The recordkeeping and paperwork added dimension to the play. Even then my right and left-brain balance was evident and so was my ability to hyper focus. I lost myself in these games that sometimes lasted several days.

As much as my mother might have complained about the disorder that my unceasing creativity caused, I think she understood my compulsion to stay busy, since she was a restless doer herself. I don't recall her ever sitting down. She tried and tried to be a good doctor's wife, decorating incessantly, painting all the rooms herself. I loved the fact that she never succumbed to the dull historical colors that were the norm, but applied her own artistic flair—cantaloupe for the hallway, moss green trim in the bathroom and marigold yellow for my bedroom. She also incorporated even more of her Italian antiques, which she mingled with accents of contemporary furniture, modern art, and worn oriental rugs. I studied all the artwork we had hanging around the house— paintings and prints from Paul Klee, Matisse and Miro, stone sculptures and quirky collages from her talented artist friends.

She herself began sculpting lessons when I was about eight or nine. I was intrigued one day when she brought me to visit her instructor Mary who lived in a revamped chicken coop on the outskirts of town.

"You mean she really lives in a chicken coop? Are there chickens there?" I couldn't imagine what kind of person would live like that.

"No, Darling. There are no chickens. It is her art studio. I just adore unconventional people, the ones who can make a home out of the most unusual buildings. You'll love it, too. And I can show you what I have been working on. It's not very good, but I enjoy learning from Mary."

Mary's home and studio captured my heart. I fantasized living in a place like this someday. It was an integrated space—her studio adjacent to a living area that was warm and inviting with open shelves of handmade pottery, houseplants and lots of books. She was a bit odd, blunt-cut graying hair, big hands and a shy laugh. She welcomed us, made tea, and then took me around the studio to show me her work and the pieces that Lucia had made.

My mother had focused her clay modeling on her favorite subject—me. There were small studies in white plaster of a young girl—lying on her stomach reading a book, sitting cross legged on the floor, relaxing, elbow on her knee. A half-sized version of my head was sculpted out of clay, a decent likeness especially the upturned corners of my lips, which mother often spoke about lovingly.

It was interesting for me to see what kind of passion was stirred up for her by these creative endeavors. She threw herself into crafting hooked rugs and silver jewelry, but none of it was what you would expect. The rug I remember best, which took her months to complete, was an abstract composition of organic shapes in shades of purple, olive, mustard and fuchsia, a completely departure from the heritage of colonial motifs that were typical of this genre. Her jewelry was amazing—oversized and bold, a juxtaposition of hammered silver with a chunk of ivory or enormous amber beads, almost tribal in design. I admired her work and so did Frank, my stepfather. I see now that, while his perceived stability drew her to marry him, it was her unconventional imagination that liberated him from his tendency to live a rigid and circumscribed life.

This unlikely pairing created a rich and interesting home life that ran the gamut between sophisticated, slightly offbeat dinner parties that my mother gave and weekends in the back field playing touch football or target shooting with Frank. He was an avid hunter, which riled my mother, who hated guns and killing and resisted anything that resembled a traditional American pastime. She complained bitterly during hunting season, but Frank just shrugged it off. This became their usual pattern: Mom finding fault and complaining, Frank smoothing out her moods without really acquiescing. I was often caught in the middle. But when it became too much, I almost always chose Frank's side. Her bickering got on my nerves.

Eventually, I made friends at school, and over the years, I became involved in all kinds of extracurricular activities—student council, cheerleading, art lessons, Girl Scouts, even a couple of church-sponsored groups, which was against Mom and Frank's strict "no religion" policy. They were both atheists and I was raised in a house where it was okay to swear, but not okay to pray to God. My Girl Scout career ended early when my mother decided it was a fascist organization and persuaded me to drop out.

Later, during my teenage years, our unconventional household became a great attraction for my friends. But when I was young, it was an embarrassment. I didn't realize then that being like everybody else meant turning my back on who I was.

My elementary school was small. The town itself was under-populated, boasting it had more cows than people. That made it relatively easy for me to stand out and succeed. I was on the honor roll, cheerleading squad, participated in school plays and gave a speech at our eighth-grade graduation. But no matter how much I explored other arenas, I never abandoned my love of art and my parents made sure I didn't.

When I was in eighth grade, I brought home a list of questions we had to fill out for our modest typewritten, mimeographed yearbook. I knew what my favorite song was and what my hobbies and sport preferences were, but I took the question of what I wanted to be when I grew up very seriously, consulting my parents one night after dinner.

"Well, if you could be anything you wanted, what would that be?" asked Frank, certain that I would choose art.

I closed my eyes and imagined my adult self. "A designer," I replied.

"What would you like to design?" he persisted, asking me to be more specific.

I thought a little harder.

"Textiles. I'd like to be a textile designer."

This was a total surprise, even to me. I had never thought of this before and don't know why it occurred to me then.

As soon as I said it, it felt right. The decision settled into my psyche for a long dormancy, but the seed was planted.

There it was—a dream sent out into the universe—destined to come back to me, decades later, long after my conscious mind had forgotten.

Besides art, nature played a large role in my spiritual and creative development. When I wasn't drawing, I was wandering around in the woods building makeshift huts and shelters out of branches and fallen pieces of wood, revealing an early impulse for seeking and designing my personal space. I fell under the spell of the surrounding forests and meadows where I lived, walking every inch of our forty acres.

My affinity for the outdoors and unspoiled wilderness made it hard for me during the summers and vacations I spent with my father and his family in New York City. I had become a country girl, and the fast pace, dirty streets and urban playgrounds felt alien to me. When I went to spend the required three weeks in summer at my father's in Manhattan, I passed much of the time sitting on the back, fire escape of my father and stepmother Gilda's fourth floor walkup, feeling bereft and alone.

The time I spent in Manhattan, however, allowed me to become close to my grandparents who lived in what seemed to be a very elegant building on East 37th street. (Since then, I have lived in the same neighborhood, and the building is actually pretty ordinary.)

My grandmother Rose was a professional woman, with an important position as National Display Director at Lerner Shops, where she presided for forty years, eventually retiring at age eighty. She was a force to be reckoned with. Used to being the boss, she pushed everybody around—her maids, her employees, and her family. She had a full-blown rivalry going with her sister, Sophie who was equally wealthy and successful in her own right. Sophie was a self-taught portrait photographer with a studio in Rockefeller Center, and she proudly drove her own Rolls Royce Silver Cloud back and forth from New York to her estate in Croton-on-Hudson. My father tells me she was the only photographer ever to capture Albert Einstein in a tuxedo.

More than once, I acted as mediator when an argument arose between Rose and Sophie. One day, when I was only nine years old, Sophie came for a family party at my grandparent's country house in Connecticut. As usual, Rose was flustered with the meal preparation, running late and ordering people around the kitchen as company began to arrive. She was always like that until someone put a cocktail in her hand, and she would then join her guests, leaving the meal-in-progress to be dealt with later. Her method of cooking involved frequent tastings, so she was never hungry, but the rest of us were ravenous, as she greeted her friends and mingled animatedly, until one of us would remind her about dinner. Often, she brought her maid Lucy, so the meal actually was served at a reasonable hour.

But this summer party had no Lucy to manage the practical aspects and Rose was in charge. Some silly fight about how to carve the roast or serve the potatoes erupted; Sophie took offense and went to sulk in her Rolls.

I volunteered to soothe her bruised ego and bring her back to the party. With a combination of flattery and pleading, I was able to coerce her to return and the day was saved. But the conflict between them continued for years, and I never understood why two sisters would let their pride drive them apart.

As difficult as Rose could be at times, we had an unusually close relationship. I spent vacations at her apartment in New York and frequent weekends at the country house in Connecticut. Now and then we even traveled to Europe together. She approached her life with unrestrained enthusiasm—everything was "just *marvelous*"—and I, as her granddaughter, felt the laser-focus of her love when I needed it most. She recognized in me not just a talent for art, but a spark of the same ambition that fueled her.

My favorite memory that illustrates this is of the time she "hired" me to do a drawing for her back-to-school window displays. I did a childlike magic marker sketch with vibrant colors and wondered how it would be used. I knew there were dozens of Lerner stores in every major city across America—the thought of my art being in all of them was overwhelming. I remember my glow of pride the day she held my hand and we made the short walk to the nearby store on Fifth Avenue and I saw my drawing enlarged to poster size in the window. This experience was the first time I ever saw my artwork reproduced and it ignited in me a lifelong passion for seeing my ideas come to life.

Recently, I came across a note I wrote to my grandmother a few months after her death at age 92, when I was in my late twenties. As difficult as she was at times, this letter illustrates the impact she had in shaping my life:

November 23, 1984

Dear Gami,

I have so much I want to share with you I don't quite know where to begin. It's not easy having you gone. I am fully aware today of the numerous ways your life has touched me and I want to thank you. I am grateful for my eyes and often, even still, they are filled with your visions. Because of you, color means something different to me than to other people. Rooms rearrange themselves. Imagination runs forcefully and deep within me.

I remember days as a child, sitting at your table, surrounded by rainbows of crayons and markers, embellishing my world, kindling the spark of what is now my life's work. I only wish you were here to see it growing. Somehow you helped instill in me a strong belief that anything is possible—that I have in me the power to create what I want and to steer the course of my life in whatever way I feel I must. The tool you provided to achieve this goal was an affirmation that the most direct and effective road to success is to be unerringly true to myself—to let my own unique personal power propel me. The "guardian angel" that you described as always hovering over your shoulder guided you through a life that was extraordinary both in its length and intensity. It was punctuated by visits to other countries, enriched by many cultures, and filled by the love of a man, a family, and countless friends, all of whom were inspired by your vitality.

*I see the flow of life from you into your great
grandchildren, my two children. Remarkable.
Their innocence and sparkling, raw show of
spirit is a gift for us all and I marvel at it. Each
step they take, each leap of learning is a miracle
unfolding. My thoughts of you remind me that
the miracle continues daily and that the simple
act of LIVING FULLY is the true triumph. Thank
you.*

*Love,
Sigrid*

I have heard from many sources that a grandparent often can provide critical inspiration, guidance and stability for children in their formative years, especially when things are a little rocky. I know that I counted on her for all of that, and she needed me just as much in return. Even now, I look for that guardian angel to give me the added confidence that everything is going to be okay.

Family fortified my early childhood. But my preteen years were saved by my complete devotion to horses. My father was the first one to introduce me to riding lessons, which I took to quite naturally. I loved everything about horses—being in the barn, riding in the ring or out on the trails, handling the saddles, nuzzling the graceful curve of their necks, even shoveling out the stalls. The place where I learned to ride was very casual—we learned English and Western techniques and we progressed with very little supervision.

After a few years of lessons my stepsister Martha and I, along with a handful of other girls, agreed to work there in exchange for free riding. By the time I was thirteen, I was capable and confident on horseback and was giving pony rides, teaching basic riding lessons and taking groups out on trail rides. After hours, we often took the horses out into the gravel pits behind the stables where there were endless trails and miles of uninterrupted fields where we could gallop freely. There were no adults around even during our weekend overnight stays. Somehow, we managed to be responsible enough to book all the reservations, manage the tacking, as well as brush and cool down the horses, just as we were taught.

One weekend, we were given the responsibility of moving the horses to another farm several miles away and followed the creek on our way south. I'll never forget the feeling of taking the horses into the water while staying mounted on their backs as they swam along with the current. These were experiences I wouldn't trade for anything. I was able to navigate the confusion and disappointment that most young teenagers suffer because I had something else to engage me. I still managed to do my homework and survive middle school, as my love affair with horses took hold of my heart.

My high school years, in the wake of Woodstock, the Vietnam War, and psychedelics, marked my transformation from honor student/cheerleader to art student/hippie. I did my share of experimentation, my wildness always tempered by a sensible desire to stay healthy and productive. My friends and I entertained ourselves by packing into any one of our cars and exploring all the back roads of the surrounding countryside in a gently altered state. We listened to music—Crosby Stills and Nash, The Who, Moody Blues, The Byrds—and we lazed beside hidden streams, enjoying the blissful peace of nature all around us. It was an idyllic time in my life.

My parents were progressive and accepting, but I knew that there was always an expectation that I would perform well in school and achieve something significant in my life. We had our share of disagreements, but I was instinctively aware that they supported me for who I was, and the potential that they saw in me, despite the fact that I had the jaded attitude of an apathetic teen, which underscored my mother's edginess all the more.

There was an incident in my senior year, however, that showed how my mother advocated for me, even when I feigned indifference. I had a 1954 Volkswagen Bug that I painted taxi yellow. The interior roof was draped with fabric from an Indian print bedspread and the entire exterior of the car was adorned with hand-painted fish, birds, and other flora and fauna. All this was met with mild amusement and approval at home. But not so at Nonnewaug Regional High School in 1970. When I was not accepted to the National Honor Society, my mother was incensed. She insisted that it was because I was being discriminated against, due to my non-conformist behavior—wearing hippie clothes to school and the appearance of my car. She went so far as to take it to the ACLU. We went together to meet with an attorney to see what could be done. I sat grimly in the lawyer's office while my mother related the offensive action of my school.

I sat slumped in my chair and when asked by the ACLU attorney, "So, Sigrid, how do you feel about this?"

I shrugged. "I don't really care."

And that was that.

I know my mother was angry—so angry she didn't say a word. It was deathly quiet as we drove home, and we never spoke of it again. I never said thank you, and she gave up trying to help. I wish we could have laughed about it, but instead it drove us further apart.

When it came time to apply to college, I had only one place in mind...*RISD—Rhode Island School of Design*. I absorbed every page of the catalog, imagining myself immersed in classes such as life drawing, graphic design and art history. But here is where my small-town education failed me. Even though I had high SAT scores, decent grades and was a National Merit Scholar (not National Honor Society though!), that didn't make up for the mediocre art training I received. My portfolio was amateurish, and my drawing skills were not very polished. I didn't have the sophistication to understand how to interpret the drawing requirement either technically or conceptually, and I was rejected. It was a huge letdown, leaving me with only a handful of second choices.

I chose the easy route, staying close to home and asking very little of myself that first year. The school I picked was a little known, very conservative art school in Hamden, Connecticut. The best aspect of this year was living in New Haven, home of my father's alma mater and my first introduction to being on my own. The limited scope of the college was disillusioning, but it did expose me to the rudimentary basics of art theory and gave me a generic working knowledge of technique. The worst part was the narrow-minded curriculum and the value placed on realistic painting and commercial art, two things in which I had zero interest. My first painting class was a shock. First of all, we could only use black and white paints. The still life setups we painted from consisted of spheres, blocks and cones, clearly meant to confine us to rendering the basic forms with photographic accuracy. Taught by an ex-marine drill sergeant who obviously learned his teaching technique in the armed services, we learned by recitation. Seriously!

Forty years later, I can still remember the rules we recited every day of class:

"Background, foreground, furthest object back, working forward."

This was nothing like what I imagined art school to be, and I hated it.

The only class that I found to be truly stimulating was Art History. I loved every lecture, especially when we covered primitive art from Egypt, Africa and Ancient Greece. It was then that I fell in love with indigenous cultures. I also fell in love with a classmate who later became my husband. I noticed him when he asked a couple of insightful questions after a lecture on African art. Our mutual fascination with this subject became a link that brought us together, and we stayed close from then on.

Despite this blossoming relationship with Steve Olsen and intervals of creative stimulation at school, I decided one year there would be enough. I did some research and chose another small art school—*Montserrat School of Visual Art* in Beverly, Massachusetts—a brand new institution founded by a group of working artists from Boston committed to true creativity. It provided the rare opportunity for students to work with a professional faculty, who were passionate about their beliefs and experienced in the field. I went for my interview and realized that this spirit of innovation, individual attention and open-mindedness was exactly what I had been seeking. In September of 1972, I packed up my belongings and moved to Cape Ann, Massachusetts, where I have lived off and on ever since. Steve transferred as well, and we started a new chapter, which marked the beginning of our life together.

I plunged headlong into art student mode during my years at *Montserrat*, trying a little bit of everything—photography, painting, printmaking, composition, graphic design, life drawing, and art history. It was 100% immersion in art. I did little else, spending hours in the studio and darkroom, volunteering to hang shows and anything else that needed doing around campus. My senior year, I became teaching assistant to a revered professor,

Paul Scott, known for his unique abstract painting course called "Plasticity and Space." I loved everything about it and was deeply proud to have been selected.

Even at *Montserrat*, progressive as it was, there was a bit of a rift between the narrative painters and the more decorative artists like me. I recall being shaken after a particularly biting critique by one of my painting instructors. He asked me what the meaning of my painting was—what was my *message*? I was stumped. I had no message. I just enjoyed the juxtaposition of colors and texture and the composition of the design. To echo Calder's words, "I don't know, I just make the stuff." I knew then that I might not be viewed as a "real" artist as I progressed in my career, but I had to do what moved me and what I felt was most expressive of my unique point of view. (Even today, I have the sense that my artwork is lightweight compared to that of other painters. But now I don't really care. I do what makes me happy. And people seem to like it.)

Steve and I were the typical struggling art students in a tiny apartment, with few belongings, an old car and a dog. I was still in my late teens as we settled into a domestic way of life that felt like playing house. We fell in love with the area. Our first living quarters were a collection of three compact rooms right on Smith's Cove in East Gloucester, a stone's throw from where I later had my gallery in the Rocky Neck Artist Colony. It was thrilling to be in a historic neighborhood, which had attracted a steady stream of artists over the last century—iconic painters such as Winslow Homer, Edward Hopper, Stuart Davis, Marsden Hartley and Milton Avery.

Another artistic phenomenon that influenced me indirectly began on Cape Ann in the 1940's. *Folly Cove Designers* was a textile design collective founded by book illustrator, Virginia Lee Burton who was married to sculptor George Demetrios. From what

I know about her, she was compulsively creative, just like me. Best known for her children's books, such as *Mike Mulligan and the Steam Shovel*, she went far beyond that when she created the very successful design cooperative, which was an extension of the arts and crafts movement of that era. It began as a course that she offered aspiring designers, giving them a chance to submit their work for inclusion in the collection.

Folly Cove Designers grew to be a successful guild of women artists who produced decorative textiles from linoleum block prints, selling their home decor designs to stores such as Lord and Taylor, which boosted their reputation and increased their business. The style was very distinctive, borrowing imagery from the surrounding seascapes, fishing villages and natural environment. Dozens of women designed prints over the years, and the collection remains an iconic tribute to the beauty of nature on Cape Ann. I have always been captivated by her story and how she ignited this enterprise in a barn in the northern end of Gloucester, especially when I realized I had just moved into a house right across the street.

The rental we found on Folly Cove was in a spectacular location. Many homes like this were occupied only in the summer, making them available for winter rental at a fraction of the price a year-round home would cost. We were overjoyed to find a place with such an amazing view and a beautiful back yard that extended right to the water. It was a two-family house and both sides were often filled to capacity with a collection of young people and students like us, forming a loose commune of sorts. The disadvantage was having to move out every June and back in come September. This action came to be known as "The Cape Ann Shuffle" by our circle of friends because so many of us were going through it every year until we could afford places of our own.

We made a pleasant life for ourselves on a limited budget with few amenities. We bought our food in bulk, taking periodic trips into Boston to shop at *Erewhon*, (*nowhere* spelled backwards), the first of its kind of natural food markets in the 1970's, founded by eco-entrepreneur, Steven Hawken (of Smith and Hawken fame). We would load up a VW van with fifty-pound bags of brown rice, flour, dried fruits, nuts and granola and trek back to Gloucester. Many of our meals were shared, and I did most of the cooking, improvising dinners for whoever might show up. Vegetarian cuisine became another creative outlet for me, and I spent a lot of time in the kitchen just inventing things.

My affinity for cooking came in handy one year when our dog was hit by a car and we had no extra funds to pay the vet bill. We decided to have a lunchtime fundraiser at *Montserrat* to raise some cash. I made a huge vat of vegetarian soup, homemade sandwiches, cookies and bread. We got permission to set up right in the lobby, which was the only common area in the building at that time, usually populated by students eating, reading or chatting between classes. The faculty was just as happy as the students to have a tasty alternative to the stale bagels and snacks available on the catering truck that was our only food option on the premises. Food trucks have come a long way since those days!

We made more money in one hour than we ever expected. I can't remember—maybe thirty-five dollars, but that was a huge take for us. Our fundraiser was such a success, we were tempted to do it again. And again. So, we approached our instructors and asked if we might be able to slip out of our morning studio classes a bit early to get lunch ready every day. I think they were so desperate for decent food they agreed, and we started a regular lunch service that fed almost everyone in the school. Everything was homemade, completely natural and vegetarian. There was no kitchen there, so we brought in our camping stove, set it up on a big table and heated the soups and stews I created at home and brought in fresh every day. Spaghetti day was the biggest hit and, of course, I made my own sauce. There were jokes about the lack of meat, but everyone was thrilled to have us cooking. It became kind of a legend that faculty and students remembered for years afterwards.

By the time I graduated in 1974, I had a sense of the kind of person I was to become and the type of life I wanted to lead. I had no idea how to make a living as an artist, but the demands of adult life had not yet arrived, and I was in no hurry to grow up. There were years ahead of me, and I vowed to keep learning and trying new things. The world was also changing so fast that I felt a moral obligation to stay true to my creative ideals, and I was gaining the skills to do just that.

Living Green

Back to the Land

"We are stardust. We are golden.
And we've got to get ourselves back to the garden."
—Joni Mitchell

My roots as a hippie began long before art school. In 1969, I was only sixteen, so I missed Woodstock, but its legacy shaped me. I embraced the idealism of the sixties with a fervency that affected everything I did. I wrote poetry, marched in anti-war demonstrations, dropped acid and committed myself to what I viewed as the new consciousness. Even my parents were swayed. My mother wore bell bottoms and ethnic jewelry, took me to Richie Havens and Pete Seeger concerts, and my step-father volunteered his medical expertise during local music festivals and even went to the March on Washington in 1969.

Intellectual and political ideology is what moved them, but for me it was something more profound.

I was less an activist and more of a spiritual seeker. I hoped to discover my true self in the context of the larger universe, with guiding principles I believed had been around since the beginning of time.

I wanted to connect with people, with nature, and with a deeper sense of purpose. The hippie movement represented an expansiveness that I sensed would hold the key to fulfilling my dreams. Yes, we wore crazy clothes, and hitchhiked all over the place. We listened to Jimi Hendrix and Janis Joplin and followed the Maharishi Mahesh Yogi. But it wasn't all for show, though I will admit I loved the style of it. Tattered, faded overalls were the staple of my wardrobe, usually paired with a Mexican peasant blouse and big dangly earrings. I had an alpaca poncho I wore over everything all winter long. In my bedroom was an eclectic array of posters—a bold Matisse print from the Museum of Modern Art, album covers from the Beatles and Moody Blues mixed with artwork I had done and taped to the wall. It was one big collage.

My favorite piece was a framed poster my mother had bought for me in a shop in Greenwich Village after a trip she had taken visiting family friends in New York. She adored the brilliant tones of yellow and orange and the stylized psychedelic writing. She even had it framed for me. I loved it because every time I looked at it, it made me smile. The poster was dominated by an enormous abstract flower bud with jagged leaves intertwined with ornate letters spelling out "Acapulco Gold." Lucia had unwittingly decorated my walls with a pot poster.

My friends and I were idealists, dreaming of a world where people lived in harmony and didn't just exist to accumulate possessions. For me, it wasn't a huge departure from the progressive way I was brought up. But for most children of that era, this new wave forced them to separate from their upbringing and establish new families, new tribes that subscribed to an alternate view of the world.

It was a powerful time in my life; one where my most deep-seated beliefs were formed. Now that I have experienced the highs and lows of life as an adult, they are no less valid. I find myself attracted to people that have some residue of that era—an intuitive kinship that I can naturally sense. So what if we are now middle-aged? The spirit of our youth still can be summoned, our minds can still expand.

In fact, I think we crave it even more now. We humans have more in common than we think. Basic principles like generosity, respect, honesty, empathy, kindness, cooperation, tolerance and thirst for learning are the values we teach our children, but then so easily abandon when we grow up. I still embrace the tenets that were the foundation of the sixties, but I understand better how to temper them with compassion and a sense of inclusiveness.

My first wedding illustrates just how homespun my life was in 1974. Just after graduating from art school, Steve and I were married in a barefoot ceremony in the back yard of the house we shared with a group of friends on Folly Cove. I was twenty years old. Our announcement elicited a mixed reaction from my relatives. When we shared the news with my Dad's side of the family over drinks at my grandparents' Murray Hill apartment, there was a round of toasts. Everyone was delighted. The fact that Steve was Scandinavian was a huge plus, even though he was Norwegian, not Danish. Lots of drinks and *skoals* were shared. If anyone was concerned that we were too young, they never said anything.

But I dreaded telling my mother. Her reaction was much as I expected.

"Sigrid," she moaned, "Why can't you just live together? You don't have to get *married*, you know."

I fumed, thinking she was being characteristically negative and unreasonable, but of course I see now that her reaction made sense. Neither of us had jobs, nor did we have a plan for the future. It just seemed like a good idea to us at the time, a good excuse for a party with our friends. We had lived together three years already, so the urgent intensity of first love had faded a bit, but we both felt ready to take the leap into our future. As usual, I was impatient to get started.

Our wedding was casual and spontaneous, largely unplanned. The ceremony itself was postponed by two hours because we were running late. At ten-thirty, I was still dressed in sweats, arranging flowers I had bought just that morning at the florist. We were forced to call the justice of the peace and ask him to come at one o'clock instead of eleven as we had planned.

It was early May and the lilacs were in bloom, but the ocean air was brisk as the motley assemblage of guests gathered on the back lawn. Steve looked like Jesus with his dark beard, long ponytail and cream-colored rustic cotton tunic. He was cold and uncomfortable in the damp shirt, which had still not dried after being washed the night before. He waited for me to get ready as more people started to arrive. My dress was hand-sewn by my friend Linda Anne out of ivory cotton eyelet in a style with soft puffed sleeves, a tie at the back and a wide ruffle at the hem. I remember scraping together the $30 she charged me for making it, which seemed like a lot at the time, but she did a beautiful job. I wore a handmade crown of flowers on my head and carried a mixed bouquet that I had fashioned myself that morning. Steve had crafted a ring with a moonstone in a silver setting he soldered himself, which was appropriately simple and beautiful until the stone fell out and was lost a few weeks later.

Both our families were in attendance, even my grandmother Rose, who was in a tizzy because we refused all her offers to give us a real wedding. She had to adjust her vigorous party planning instincts to adapt to what we wanted—an informal potluck dinner with friends. She insisted on providing the wine and traditional Danish *kransekake*, my favorite dessert (a "crown" made from tiers of concentric rings of almond flavored cookies, covered in Danish and American flags). She fussed about, decorating tables, arranging wine bottles, trying in vain to formalize the soiree, but eventually she calmed down and enjoyed herself. Once our guests began to appear with warm loaves of homemade bread, she and my mother both began to relax and embrace the free spirit of the celebration.

When I dashed across the lawn, I was barefoot, arm-in-arm with my father, who looked striking in his bright red jacket and pink shirt with a colorful tie. I was happy to have him by my side, and he, just like in every social occasion, was beaming and full of joy. As we approached the circle of people who had formed in the backyard for the ceremony, I was told that Ken, our quirky but lovable friend, who lived nearby in an odd hexagonal house he designed and built himself, had an idea for the ceremony.

"Okay," I thought. "I guess it's a good thing somebody has a plan."

He pulled us aside and explained. "I have given a daisy to each of the guests. As soon as the vows are finished, each of the men will come up to Sigrid and give her their flower and then the women will do the same for Steve."

Steve and I exchanged a look, both a little worried our families would feel awkward with this. I was slightly irritated that he had taken it upon himself to impose his idea on our wedding, plus it seemed a little hokey to me, but I had no plan, so I nodded my head and we proceeded. The flower exchange broke the ice nicely, after all. Even the more conservative family members ended up surrendering to the craziness of the entire day and just had fun.

The wedding was simple and unconventional and so was our brief honeymoon. We agreed what we really wanted to do was take our new down sleeping bags (the one wedding gift we had requested) across the street into the woods for a single night of camping under the stars. The evening was uneventful. We had slept in these woods before and would do it again. Waking up the next morning, we returned to our normal routine. We were married, but nothing felt much different. I think I was a little disappointed that it wasn't more romantic, but we were both exhausted from the day's activities and focused instead on the life we had to look forward to. This offbeat way of doing things was typical of the years that followed, a foreshadowing of our slightly haphazard and improvised life together.

Even before we were married, we talked about finding a piece of land somewhere to make a homestead where we would build a dwelling, grow our own food and live a simple life. We had already done a little research during the past couple of years to see what we could find, exploring the coast from Maine to the Carolinas. On one trip, we took a route through the Blue Ridge Mountains and the panoramic countryside of rural Virginia. It was truly breathtaking. We had no idea how this trip would figure into our long-term plans, but we were open to anything.

"Wow," said Steve as we made our way through velvety green rolling hills, dotted with small farms, horse pastures and virgin forest. "I would love to find a place to buy here. Imagine the gardens we could have, and there is plenty of space for animals. Let's get off the main road and do a little investigating."

We drove through the lush green Fort Valley, which sat nestled within the Shenandoah Valley, about three hours from

Washington, D.C. It was sparsely inhabited, really off the beaten track. I was wondering if we would find anyone who had interests in common with two art students from Massachusetts, but Steve was more positive.

"Look. There is a sign that says *Frogmoor Farm, Nubian goats.* Let's check it out." He had read about this breed, which was originally from Africa and had a sweet look because of their floppy ears. They were also great milk producers, and we had become fond of goat's milk, which was only available in health food stores at that time. Steve was constantly reading about anything and everything and became obsessed with the idea of raising goats.

We meandered down a long serpentine driveway that led to a tidy white farmhouse and several outbuildings on a huge spread of land with a small pond in the distance. We were met outside the barn by David, the owner, a trim, neatly dressed older gentleman, who had bought the farm a few years prior and was gradually improving and grooming the property. A retired parasitologist from Washington, D.C., he had moved here to perfect his animal husbandry techniques and to raise prizewinning Nubian goats. His meticulousness was apparent in the carefully maintained grounds and sterile conditions of the barns and dairy facilities.

"Nice place you have here," Steve was admiring the spread as I stood back, wondering what it would be like to live in such a beautiful, but out of the way location. "We are just passing through but saw your sign. We were hoping to buy a little goat's milk from you."

It was obvious we weren't from around there. The shabby foreign car, bohemian attire, long hair, frisky dog with a bandana collar—these were not common sightings in this valley, not to mention the fact that he knew everyone who lived there, and they knew him as well. When strangers entered Fort Valley, everybody knew. I felt shy, like we were intruders, but Steve was deep in conversation with David, asking questions about the farm and how he raised his goats, and giving him a little bit about our background. He said we were from the coast of Massachusetts, art students, he worked as a carpenter—all the basic points—leaving out the more controversial aspects of our anti-establishment belief system.

Somehow, Steve won him over because he warmed up to us and straightforwardly asked:

"I am looking for help here at the farm. You seem to like goats. It's hard work, but maybe you would be interested? I can't pay you, but I can put you up here at the house and show you around the area. I have a piece of property just over the hill that could use some fixing up."

Steve and I looked at one another, intrigued. We took a moment to talk about the prospect.

I was honest with Steve about my feelings, encouraging this as a first step toward our dream. "This is just the kind of place we have been looking for and maybe we aren't quite ready to do this by ourselves just yet anyway." I think that having someone else in charge made me feel safe, less vulnerable. After all I was just out of my teens at this point, not prepared to be completely on my own.

Steve was game, as usual. "Let's say yes. How bad could it be? We love animals, the place is beautiful and we can plant a garden. It will give you time to do your art work and if we end up with our own piece of property, that's great. Plus, the climate is warmer than where we are now."

After this excursion, we returned home to Cape Ann, packed up our belongings—art supplies, garden tools, eight harness loom, Steve's carpentry tools and our black lab Josh—into our old Peugeot station wagon and made the return trip south to the small town of Seven Fountains, Virginia, with high hopes to start the new life we'd dreamt of.

Returning to the secluded Fort Valley where the goat farm was located, we were reminded of the natural beauty of the area we had chosen for our new home. When we arrived at the farm, David greeted us again warmly. As we took in our new surroundings and wandered the premises for a second time, we must have seemed a little dazed to him. It surprised me that he accepted the two of us— so different from him or anyone else in the valley—into his rarified realm. But now that I look back on it with an unvarnished eye, who else would be willing to work in this godforsaken wilderness in exchange for room and board in a farmhouse with no indoor toilet and an eccentric aging scientist for company?

We were happy at first, enchanted by the pastoral setting. The animals were frisky and adorable, and we felt lucky to have an opportunity to hang out with them on a daily basis. We were given a guest room in the main house with the renewed promise that we could purchase the neighboring parcel at a very low price if everything worked out. The farmhouse was simple but comfortable, and we got used to the outhouses, which were incredibly clean due to the fastidiousness of our host. We learned right away that scientists, especially those whose life study was about parasites and bacteria, have very high standards of cleanliness, which was a bit of an adjustment for us but not insurmountable. Our poor dog no longer was able to lick the plates clean after supper and, in general, was considered a breeding ground for disease.

Fortunately, Steve and I both had plenty of energy and physical stamina because we were busy from dawn to dusk with farm chores. The first milking was at four a.m. and the second milking exactly 12 hours later. He was a stickler about this. Why it could not have been seven a.m. and seven p.m. I have no idea because I never dared ask. David had trained us with painstaking precision, instructing us on dairy procedures and bringing us in to observe the birthing of new kids. He demonstrated just how to lead the doe onto the milking stand, tether her in and get in the proper position to do the milking by hand. Goats have two teats, not four like a cow, and the trick is to let the conical nipple fill with milk, close it off at the base and then squeeze gently, not pulling—just allowing each rhythmic compression to bring the milk down into the pail. Once it starts to flow, it is a strong and steady stream, and if the doe moves abruptly, it can get out of control easily. He watched us until he was satisfied we wouldn't damage the udder by yanking too hard and that we were getting every last drop. It took me a little while to get the hang of it, but eventually I was reasonably proficient, and I could exit the milking room without my clothes smelling like cheese.

It gave me a profound sense of tranquility to fall into the rhythm of life on a farm. There is a timelessness to tending animals. Doing such vital life tasks made me feel connected with ancient cultures and grounded to the earth. If it had just been Steve and me doing the chores, I would have been happy. But, we had to conform to the schedule and lifestyle contrived by our boss, and our life views couldn't have been more different. I started to feel too constrained, and I resented David for that.

After morning milking, it was my responsibility to make breakfast—all the meals in fact—because the women's movement apparently had not yet reached Seven Fountains, Virginia. Most days after breakfast, I experimented with uses for goat's milk—

yogurt, cheese, ice cream—because we had *so much* of it. Why? Because evidently, the way goats are judged to be champions is not just by their physical characteristics (stance, size of udder) but also the volume of their milk production. So we followed the strict protocol David prescribed. We milked the goats religiously, measured every ounce of their output, recorded it in a journal, along with the weather conditions, outside temperature and God knows what else. Then, in most cases, we threw it away. We used what we could and gave some to neighbors but, because it was unpasteurized, it was illegal to sell it. I am positive there was no cleaner dairy farm in a hundred-mile radius, but that was the law. This fact alone began to chip away at my dream of staying here forever. Instead of living off the land as we hoped, we were just caught in a competition for show. We hauled bales of hay, tilled the soil and cared for the animals. For what? To boost David's ego, enabling him to win ribbons at the State Fair and be written up in farm journals.

But that wasn't all. It was lonely and isolating in this remote valley, away from the community of close friends we had made in Massachusetts. My creative nature collided with the strictly scientific approach we were forced to take about everything at the farm—in the kitchen, in the barn, in conversations at the dinner table.

I decided one day to break out of my routine and try to make some friends in the surrounding area. I joined the Junior League. A few local women invited me to a meeting one day, so I agreed to go. I am sure they viewed me as an oddity in their midst. They had probably heard of hippies but had never actually met one. Now I know why we were called freaks. What seemed normal to me was, in fact, a complete aberration for much of society in 1974. Especially for the nice ladies of Seven Fountains.

Blissfully unaware of the dress code for Junior Leaguers, I showed up in my usual garb—tiered cotton skirt, embroidered peasant blouse, bare unshaven legs in chunky hiking boots and my hair in Heidi braids pinned to the top of my head. Most of the ladies in attendance were wearing cardigans and pearls. Their homes were unlike any I had seen up north—lazy boy recliners, polished TV consoles, matching upholstery, plastic tablecloths, silk flowers, knickknacks everywhere—no books, no paintings, and certainly no indigenous textiles or hand thrown pottery, like I was brought up with. Still, they were kind to me in their sweet Southern way, and I relished even the most tenuous connection with other women my age. Just like when I was a child, I was eager to be accepted and happy to play, no matter what the circumstance.

Only one of the Junior League members was someone I could call a friend. Her name was Meg, and she had moved there with her family from D.C., believing it was a healthier place to raise their two small children. Her husband was a photojournalist for National Geographic, and when I visited her, I was impressed by the collection of books, magazines and photography they had in their home. It felt good there, a comforting mix of homey, handcrafted quilts and needlepoint with tasteful paintings, prints and shaker furniture. It was the one and only time that I felt a cultural kinship there in the valley, and the connection made me believe I might be able to stay. I felt Meg had an inkling of what made me tick, how art and culture were important to me, and she had a sense that it might be hard for me to find my place in this backwoods community. I thought: "If she can do it, then I can." But the truth was, I didn't fit in. Meg was more conservative than I ever would be, and I found it increasingly difficult to compromise and adapt.

My creative drive was set aside for the time being, except for one thing...our garden. It was enormous. Maybe 600 square feet, all tilled, composted, planted and cultivated by the two of us. There was no running water close to the field where we planted, so we watered the garden daily with buckets we hauled up from a nearby stream. I pored over books, read Organic Gardening Magazine and the Whole Earth Catalog avidly, gleaning anything I could about the secrets of successful horticulture without pesticides and synthetic fertilizer. One method, called "companion planting" suggested placing certain crops together to ward off insects—nasturtiums and cucumbers, marigolds and tomatoes, petunias and pole beans. I spent hours drawing diagrams of garden plans in my sketchbook, imagining the amazing effect that mingling flowers and vegetables would have on the garden design. All the rows emanated from a central ring of vibrant flowers that encircled a mound of lettuces in brilliant shades of green. The pole beans wound their tendrils around the teepees we made of cut branches and, when they bloomed, the tiny pink sprays of pea blossoms were a beautiful contrast to the purple petunias at their feet. My Junior League lady friends came to visit one day and declared our garden "just as pretty as a picture," since they had never seen anyone plant anything but straight rows and never flowers and vegetables mixed together. I loved looking at it as much as eating from it. Maybe more.

The visual impact of horticulture seeped into my artwork. Green has remained my favorite color—not emerald or British racing green but the rich vital green of new leaves imbued with sunlight, the shimmering translucent evidence of photosynthesis. This hue was the backdrop, accented by all the beautiful blossoms and vegetables that grew heartily throughout. The inspiration fed my soul while we toiled, and it made me happy to have my hands in the dirt.

We tended the garden with loving attention in our off hours, which weren't very plentiful. At night there was no TV or radio.

We would read, and sometimes, I would weave on my loom or draw in my sketchbook. But by the time the summer twilight had faded to night, we usually faded, too, exhausted from the day's labor, resting up for the next one.

It was certainly a crash course in animal husbandry, and there were times I really loved it.

Mornings were magical—the sun, timid at first, would break through wide cracks between the barn boards and shed golden light onto the hay where the baby goats were sleeping.

The minute they heard us approach they would jump up, their hooves pounding on the wood of their stalls like frantic door knockers, and bleat pitifully to tell us they were hungry. Instead of nursing directly from their mothers, the babies were taken away and bottle-fed so that we could monitor the does' milk production more accurately. I found this to be incredibly sad and unnecessarily cruel, but like most children, they simply adjusted to the life they were given.

I, however, was not adjusting to our new life so well. It was more like 4H and less like Woodstock, as I had hoped. I knew of 4H from my rural upbringing—a worldwide organization that promoted agriculture for young people with four guiding principles: head, heart, health and hands. It always seemed like a wholesome idea, but I never envisioned myself joining an organization like that to get close to the earth. I was always more drawn to the counterculture than the mainstream.

I had thought living so close to nature in such a beautiful place would satisfy me, but it wasn't enough. This was my first lesson in the importance of cultural stimulation and collective consciousness. Higher awareness did not necessarily accompany life in a bucolic environment. By the time three months had passed, I was ready to go home. Back to people who shared my progressive values and offbeat fashion sense, back to potluck dinners with my friends from the food co-op, back to painting and drawing and craft shows and galleries. Back to my tribe.

Steve was more malleable, but he recognized we were fish out of water, too. I think he would have gone anywhere that he could be close to animals and use his hands to create. Ultimately, we were both glad to get back to people we cared about and with whom we had a long history. We looked at our time in Virginia as a summer project, a three-month experiment where we gained experience and knowledge, it was rigorous training for the future, especially if we planned to tend the land and live in the country. Now, we had many more tools under our belt.

David was surprised at our decision, as is often the case with people who are so internally focused they have no sense of others' emotions. If he had paid attention at all, he would have known that we were growing increasingly disenchanted and distant. If he felt hurt or angry, he didn't say so. He just wished us well, and we were on our way.

We left the farm with a couple of baby goats as payment for our work and arrived back on Cape Ann in time for autumn in New England. We had no money and no jobs, so we spent the winter living in my father's country house in Connecticut, while he was ensconced with his new family in New York. It worked out nicely for all of us. We kept an eye on his and my grandmother's houses, which were less than a mile apart and were able to save some money to help us get back to Cape Ann the next summer. We tended our goats and took odd jobs as they came by. Steve honed his carpentry skills, and I went to work in a local health food store, which I loved. Still, we longed for the community we had left behind. So before long, we made our way back to the place and people who had established a home in our hearts.

Geographically, Cape Ann is an island connected to the mainland by two bridges. About fifty minutes north of Boston, it is the lesser known Cape, Cape Cod being much more popular. It contains two towns: Gloucester, a city of about 30,000 and Rockport, a quaint fishing village on the northeast side with a population of nearly 7,000 that swells to about twice that in the summertime. The perimeter of the island is rimmed by a main road with various small streets extending off of it. The center of this land mass is called Dogtown and is largely uninhabited.

Dogtown has its own mythology and history, but to me it's simply a beautiful, unspoiled woodland with a crisscross of intersecting trails connecting all my friends to each other. We each lived in various corners of the Cape and were so familiar with the paths that led to one another's houses, we could walk them in the dark. I remember taking exuberant hikes on snowy, moonlit nights and meditative daily treks from my little house in the woods to my studio, through forests of silver beech trees and striking stands of white birch. During the summer, I would throw a book and blanket in my backpack and hop on my bike to sunbathe for a few hours on the rocky shoreline and dip into the frothy sea. It felt wild and untainted by modern civilization. Nature at its best.

Years went by, and we both expanded our skills, taking all sorts of jobs; I, a Montessori teaching assistant, nutritional counselor in a chiropractor's office and adult education instructor, teaching courses as diverse as silk screening, weaving and natural food cooking, while Steve continued to master carpentry and began to specialize in boat building.

We moved from place to place. One summer, we were in-between houses, so we built a lean-to on a friend's land. It was on the edge of a quarry not far from our previous home in Folly Cove. With a few hanging baskets, canning jars filled with cut wildflowers, and a bowl of fruit on a makeshift table, it was home for a few months.

Eventually, we took over the rental of a very rustic little house in the woods from a friend. It was situated down a long dirt road in Pigeon Cove, a sparsely settled corner of Rockport where no one seemed to notice that we were living without running water or electricity. We paid sixty dollars a month and our other expenses were minimal. We jokingly called it "Dogpatch" after the Kentucky hillbilly town from the Lil Abner comic strip. It looked very much like it.

My first introduction to the place had been a few years before this when our friends who lived there invited us for Thanksgiving dinner. We walked over through the woods from our place in Folly Cove on a damp and chilly November afternoon. We entered the house just as the holiday dinner was being served—a humongous Hubbard squash with an uncanny resemblance to an actual roast turkey, and I got a taste of my first vegetarian Thanksgiving dinner.

There was something otherworldly about the whole experience—the sense that we were adventurers living an alternate lifestyle on the same planet we had inhabited since birth, but in a world that was completely different from the one in which we were raised. We were paving a new road, and it seemed it would take us anywhere we wanted.

Our life in the woods may have seemed simple, but in many ways, it was more complicated. The tasks of daily life became the center of our existence. Chop firewood for the wood stove. Haul water from the cistern in the cellar for washing dishes. Stock up on ice for the "ice box", keep the kerosene lanterns filled, get food at the Co-op, carry bottles to the spring for drinking water. We had three choices when it came time for a shower. One: heat water on the stove and fill the galvanized tub in the yard. Or two: walk up the road to a friend's house, towel in hand. Or three: shower after a swim at the Y. One winter the snow was so deep we gave up trying to drive in. We parked the car in a small lot on the main road and cross-country skied in and out on a daily basis, even with laundry and groceries.

When my mother came to visit us, she was forced to stay in a nearby hotel and whine, "Why are you doing this to me, Sigrid?" I tried to accommodate her, always aware that her standard of living was so vastly different from the one I had chosen, but this comment was so typically narcissistic, it grated on me, and I couldn't help but react. "I didn't do this *to you*, Mom. It's the way we have chosen to live. You don't have to live here. I wish you would just accept it and enjoy the time we have together, instead of wasting time complaining."

She blamed Steve. "How can your husband let you live like this?"

"What? It is as much my decision as his. I like it here. I don't want the same things you want."

No matter how many years went by, even in my more conventional abodes, I always got irritable before she came to visit. I spent days cleaning, self-conscious about my secondhand furniture and piles of debris everywhere. And then at a certain point, about twenty years later, I understood. I can't pinpoint the exact moment that my income and lifestyle surpassed my parents, but it was remarkable and strange. It seemed like one day I was ashamed of my dirty, unfinished house, and resentful that they could pay for whatever they needed—furniture, repairs, pretty things—and the next I was living on the forty-fifth floor of a Manhattan highrise with a grand piano and unobstructed sunset views of the Empire State building. Lucia loved that apartment and visited often, never complaining about a thing. But that was years later. I had no clue that someday I would earn my own living and rise to a level that could satisfy even my mother's refined tastes.

For the few years we lived at Dogpatch, I wore it proudly like a badge. There was something about the subsistence lifestyle that felt like a huge accomplishment. Who knows? Maybe I was living like this for the precise reason that my mother would never have chosen it for me. But, at the time, I truly enjoyed the mindfulness required to attend to our daily life.

I approached the most basic household task as though it was a meditation. We had a hand-powered, stone grinder fastened to the kitchen counter, which I used regularly to grind the wheat kernels we bought in fifty-pound bags to make our bread. I could make soup out of anything and often did. I learned how to use a splitting maul to chop firewood for the wood stove and even acquired the basic carpentry skills needed to erect a simple structure. (At least I know I can survive in almost any situation if I have to.)

My personal commitment to yoga was also borne out of this period, establishing the core values that molded me:

- self-reliance
- discipline
- introspection

- acceptance
- peace
- appreciation of the beauty of nature

Steve and I learned basic Hatha Yoga from a lovely young lady who had spent time on an ashram in India and brought her teachings to New Haven when we were still in college there. Years later, we studied Transcendental Meditation (TM), and received our mantras at a local TM center where we met and made friends with many members. I began to rely on my daily practice to put me in touch with a deeper sense of self and help relax me.

We both started meditating faithfully twice a day no matter where we were. Even when we visited family, we disappeared for twenty minutes before dinner to find a quiet place to practice. We discovered in our travels that even though we never went to church during services, the doors were always open, and we could duck in anytime to meditate. We did this even on the streets of New York, which made our visits to the city bearable. We had removed ourselves so far from the fast-pace of society, it set us off-kilter to be in urban surroundings, and meditation helped us stay centered.

It's incongruous to say we meditated to combat stress, because in those days, I had no idea what stress was. My life was easy, and time was abundant. Only later, when the demands of my profession were amplified to an almost unbearable volume, did I come to truly understand the antidote that yoga could provide for easing tension. It was also my way to find a kindred community that crossed all socio-economic boundaries, making me feel like we really were one, unified world. Still does.

It was indeed a spiritual quest. My mother, while impressed with the physical workout, always considered my interest in yoga and Eastern philosophy as "mystical." She truly believed religion to be the opiate of the masses and was afraid I was being brainwashed by a cult. In the greater community we were considered wayward flower children with our heads in the clouds. It's ironic to consider that my generation, steeped in the sixties counter-culture, is now all grown up. We are the establishment now.

We never anticipated how mainstream yoga would become. There was no indication that in a few decades there would be yoga studios in towns across all fifty states and organic vegetables in every supermarket. Things have really changed. All the articles about trendy styles of yoga and the benefits of meditation make it seem like these practices are relatively new. But the ancient practice has roots that are deeply spiritual and profound.

I found my place in the spiritual community of the mid-seventies, just as TM was gaining in popularity. The Maharishi Mahesh Yogi had created a worldwide craze after his appearance on the Merv Griffin Show and his affiliation with the Beatles. TM was also making headlines during that period for "Yogic Flying" which claimed that prolonged meditation sessions enabled practitioners to levitate or "hop" in a cross-legged position. I witnessed these sessions audibly during weeklong retreats that were held at a seaside hotel in Rockport during the winter of 1975. I could hear the *thump, thump, thump* of the advanced yogis during their evening sessions as they "lifted off" during meditation.

That winter I volunteered to be the chef for these events. In exchange, I would receive free tuition for a week-long meditation retreat, hoping to advance my practice to where I had an inkling of how one could learn to levitate. I had plenty of time to spare, and I grasped at any chance to be close to the TM movement and master my own practice. Also, the challenge of cooking for this particular group appealed to me. I had never cooked professionally before, but I leapt to the task with optimistic naïveté.

Alone in the big industrial hotel kitchen, I pondered my approach. I decided to give the dinner meals an international theme and each night created vegetarian menus from different countries—one night India, the next Mexico, Italy, Greece and so on. It was hard work, but creatively challenging and I reveled in the compliments and appreciation of the guests. It also reinforced my commitment to natural foods as a foundation for healthy living. (Today, creating menus to accommodate my personal food philosophy (easy/healthy/beautiful/delicious) comes naturally. It's indelibly ingrained by the things I taught myself in the kitchen during this time.)

The slower pace of my life in those days allowed me to enjoy the beauty of the changing seasons, and it affected my artwork. After college, I delved into textiles, and taught myself to weave on an eight-harness floor loom. I spun my own wool and dyed it with flowers and berries I collected outdoors. Since we had no extra space in our little house, I accepted a friend's offer to set up my loom and studio in the attic of her house a few miles away. Every day I walked through the woods to "work," inspired by the landscape. The silvery bark of a beech tree, the russet accent of red oak and the delicate, pale yellow birch leaves all found their way into the color and texture of my weavings. I loved the idea that I could create pillows and wall hangings to sell at craft shows that would bring a piece of nature into people's homes.

I felt like I was gathering up all the beauty and inspiration as a gift from the landscape and passing it on through my creations.

The travel to and from my studio took time, but the walk was part of the experience. It became just as important to me as the hours I spent working at the loom, keeping me grounded, while the fresh air enlivened all my senses. Even when I was eight months pregnant, I walked the familiar route with gratitude for such a peaceful and fulfilling life. I was satisfied for the time being.

Our first child, Erik, was born while we lived in the little house in the woods. It was a bitterly cold February night and even with the wood stove burning at an intense rate, the house was still freezing. We had planned a home birth, but after forty hours of unproductive labor, our midwives decided it was time to go to the hospital. I was disappointed, but exhausted—everyone else was, too. After a few more hours of intense labor, Erik was born, strong and healthy, and I became a mother. In one life-changing moment our small family of two had become three.

It's a miracle that happens every minute of every day around the world, yet I was completely astonished at the overwhelming wonder of bringing a new being into the world. My notion of love was redefined in an instant. Before even a day passed at the hospital, we traveled back home with our precious cargo, awed by the responsibility of caring for a new life. Steve and I kept looking at him and then at each other, smiling incessantly. I marveled at how this baby tapped into a gentleness lying dormant in Steve until he became a father.

We showed him off to everybody. My mother came to visit with her sister Franca just after he was born. They were immediately smitten, scrutinizing every feature of his little face, looking for genetic traits. They babbled animatedly in a jumble of English and Italian:

"Sigrid, he has your nose, but his eyes are more like Steve's. *Piccolo bello.*"

"*Che caro!* What about his coloring? Is he blonde? Is he dark like his father? *Prezioso!*"

"*Ma la boca, come Sigrid.* What a mouth. I remember when you were a baby, Sigrid. They would bring you to me in the hospital and when you saw me you would make a sucking sound with your little lips."

And she demonstrated, her mouth a puckered "o." This was a story she would repeat often, especially towards the end of her life when her short-term memory was gone and images from the past were all she had to keep with her in the nursing home.

Having a baby softens everyone, even if only for a short while. In Connecticut, my grandmother greeted her first great-grandchild with dramatic zeal.

"Here, let me hold him," she urged as she pressed his little body up against her gigantic bosom, beaming at his tiny face then looking up at me and winking. At dinner, my grandfather insisted on a toast, clinking his glass and raising it *"to Erik,"* impressed by the Norse name we had chosen. Lucy, my mother's Jamaican maid, who had known me since I was a baby, hugged me and pronounced in her soft Caribbean lilt, "Now you a *real wooman*, honey." I finally felt like she might be right.

I was twenty-five when Erik was born, and Steve was thirty-two. We had already been married for five years and eased into this next phase with blissful ignorance. We didn't know what we didn't know. I wrote emotional poetry about my coming of age as a mother—this one composed after both of my children were born:

> *"Tears well inside me and quietly fall in gratitude and amazement at the lives before me. I adore their innocent simplicity and ache to allow it*

to remain with them always. I imagine that they will hear the drumbeats of rain on the roof at night, let bright stars pierce their hearts, and be healed by the moon. I wish for their lives to have all the timeless texture of rocks being worn into sand by the sea, each grain a crystal reflecting the vast universe."

Both Steve and I had a romanticized vision of what it would mean to raise a child. Like most new parents, we thought our life wouldn't change much at all. And it didn't—at first.

Erik was the second child born in our close circle of friends. Linda Anne, my wedding dress seamstress, had her son a couple of years before. Steve and I were at her home birth, totally awestruck by the primal power of the event. She and her husband were vegetarians, adhering to a strict macrobiotic diet, and they approached everything, including childrearing, with almost sanctified purity. Linda Anne became a midwife herself and was installed as the director of the birth center where our daughter, Brita, was born three years later. I wasn't sure I would ever measure up to the exemplary regimen that Tucker and Linda Anne practiced, but it influenced me, and I tried very hard to follow the laws of nature with my own parenting.

The days after Erik's birth passed quietly as I adjusted to life as a new mother—breastfeeding, massaging his tiny baby body by the warmth of the wood stove, taking long walks to the sea with my tightly wrapped bundle in a *Snugli*. Every evening, I would heat water on the kitchen stove and give him a warm bath in a galvanized tub placed atop a metal stand that stood table height right next to the counter where I was preparing dinner. He splashed and played while I cooked. Multi-tasking already came naturally to me. I found these domestic rituals comforting, and for once, I was calm and patient while the days flowed by.

Nothing lasts forever.

Eventually during my evening walks, I found myself peering with envy into neighbors' windows that radiated with the warm golden glow of electric lights. I tired of hauling laundry in and out and having to use the outhouse in the middle of winter. So eventually, we pooled our resources and found a house we could afford on Main Street in Rockport. It was quite a step—joining the mainstream, living in a real house and becoming part of the provincial community of small town New England. Before long, we had a second child, Brita, and settled into a new life with Steve working at a boat yard while I set up a studio in the upstairs of our barn.

Then our friends began to have babies. Children were being born all around me and suddenly I was immersed in a maternal community that provided all the support I needed. Being connected to other adults is a *must* when one's days are filled with changing diapers, reading stories, feeding, nursing and baby talk. One of our most ambitious endeavors was to create a local Mother's Center where women could go to meet one another, lessening feelings of isolation and loneliness that so easily arise after becoming a new parent. I luxuriated in the warmth and encouragement of this sisterhood and there are elements of this type of connection that have resurfaced frequently for me over the years. I felt this support enabled me to better appreciate and enjoy the slower pace of life with children, and it gave me a sense of purpose to be part of an extended communal family committed to helping one another.

It took a little organization to make it happen. A few of us persevered until we secured a venue in the Episcopal Church basement, and those more diligent activists among us researched a feminist curriculum to use as a guide for our services. I had my hands full with two kids and was better suited to the interpersonal, creative stuff that leaned more towards potluck dinners and greeting newcomers. We had support groups for pregnant women, mothers of newborns, toddlers, even teenagers, though there were few of us in that category. The stepparents' group was one of the first of its kind, most of us were still on our first marriages then and imagined we would stay there forever, though the majority of us did not. We shared tips on breastfeeding, exchanged recipes and provided childcare while women participated in the groups. For many new mothers, this was the only respite they had from the unceasing duty of motherhood.

This was years before I became a working mother with a fulltime job and none of my friends worked in the traditional sense of the word. In some ways the demands of this life far outweighed a nine-to-five job, but we reveled in the notion that we were all in it together. The solidarity was a comfort.

I still had trouble taking it easy. I was always busy and slightly overcommitted. I joined all kinds of groups in addition to the Mother's Center. I became involved in our local Food Coop and eventually served as President for a short time. Joining the Cape Ann Artisans kept my creative spirit alive, and I volunteered for various tasks there as well. I still tried to spend time working in my studio any chance I got and bonded with other mothers who did the same. I was habitually productive and determined that motherhood wasn't going to interfere with my compulsion. I needed it like a drug. I approached everything from this angle, which made my life messy but interesting.

One year, I decided I would make winter jackets for my two little ones. The construction was very simple since I had only the most rudimentary sewing skills. I went to Chinatown in Boston and bought some wool remnants and an old fur jacket at a thrift store. Cutting out the pattern pieces by eye, I fashioned jackets out of six basic rectangles—two for the front, one for the back, two sleeves and a hood. I edged the hood with a strip of fur from the old jacket. The buttons were slices of an apple tree branch that I cut on Steve's band saw, smoothed with sandpaper and drilled with two holes. I worked quickly, impatiently, and had them both done in a day or two. I'm not sure how practical they were, but they looked adorable. Thus began my penchant for fashion.

I still loved growing things, but my new garden was modest compared to the one we had cultivated in Virginia. A few patches of strawberries and rows of lettuce, peppers, beans and tomatoes in our back yard were all we could manage. I still planted flowers, but they were sparse in comparison to the bounty of our showcase garden.

The year I was pregnant with Brita, I did my best to prepare for spring planting. It wasn't easy while managing an active toddler and a house that seemed to be in a constant state of disarray. I diligently started my vegetables from seed in small flats and waited for them to sprout in the sun outside in the yard.

There was an incident involving Erik and my baby seedlings that has become a family favorite since my father, the cinematographer, captured it on film. It was a short piece entitled *Erik and Friends*, a home movie that was remarkable at the time but today would be just an ordinary video captured on a smart phone. It also reveals a bit of my father's journalistic detachment as well as his quietly sinister sense of humor.

The scene: mid-afternoon on a cool spring day. Our messy back yard is littered with toys, tools and flats of vegetable seedlings waiting to be planted. Erik awakens from his nap and appears at the screen door, grumpy, still drowsy, waiting to be let outside. You can hear multiple high-pitched greetings from the family, coaxing him to smile, but he remains stone-faced. Once out on the back step, he lurches, almost drunkenly, through the yard leading my father, camera-in-hand, to the far end of our property to visit a horse that lives in a barn behind us, murmuring "horsey" as he stumbles through the deep grass, tripping occasionally over branches in his way. Shortly, we see him toddle back into view with his grandfather close behind. The film cuts to me as I appear just in time to see Erik sawing through the stems of all of my green pepper plants with a plastic butter knife while everyone else stands by to watch. I gape in horror, utter a curse word, turn to my father, furious, as the camera keeps rolling. When I realize I am being filmed, I quickly censor myself. It's a classic—one Erik enjoyed reliving all his life and kept to show his own children, and one that made my father laugh heartily any time it was mentioned.

This is a perfect example of the "one step forward-two steps back" kind of progress (or lack of) that happens when you are a young parent. I was equally committed to childrearing and holding true to my personal vow to stay close to the earth, keeping nature at the center of my family's life. I tried to instill a reverence for the outdoors, which I see reflected, not just in my children, but in my grandchildren as well. I had to smile when one day, during a visit with Erik at his home in Vermont. I drove my seven-year-old granddaughter Mia to school and, looking up at the clouds, she spontaneously said, "I just love nature, don't you, Nona?"

Artisan Entrepreneur

"Do not go where the path may lead.
Go instead where there is no path and leave a trail."
—Ralph Waldo Emerson

As an artist with two small children, I struggled to balance my maternal instincts with a nearly constant stream of creative activities. Learning the skill of multi-tasking was essential for me to manage a life that was always slightly on the verge of catastrophe. Everything I attempted had to be accomplished in small, hour-long increments, while my kids were napping or at preschool. I was a weaver, a painter, a community organizer, a wife and mother. So many roles, so little time. Compelled to create, it was about this time I discovered a new textile medium that would completely change everything.

As a weaver, I had already become disenchanted. I was simply too impatient. The tedium of hand-weaving was getting old, and I was on the edge of boredom. It took too long to thread the loom, and I found the slow pace of sending the shuttle across the warp just to make a few inches of fabric increasingly tiresome. Eventually, it overshadowed the joy that attracted me to the craft in the first place: working with gorgeous home spun yarns in their beautiful array of colors. The love of textiles still drew me, I just needed to figure out how to satisfy the flow of ideas with something that would be quicker and more productive.

I discovered textile design through trial and error. I had always loved printmaking—it was my major focus in college—and had played around with potato printing a few times, making Christmas cards and wrapping paper. Something about the process of carving designs out of an actual potato, carefully stamping images into a repeated pattern and getting immediate results, appealed to me. It seemed so organic, almost primordial. And it was quick.

It occurred to me that if I substituted textile silkscreen inks for the traditional block printing inks I could print fabric with the same potato stamps that I had used to decorate my holiday cards. With just a small paring knife, I carved a diverse library of shapes that I would use in my prints—birds, fish, leaves, flowers, clouds, water, sailboats, hills and palm fronds. They were completely unique, a product of my imagination, carved in relief onto the flat surface of a potato.

The geometric patterns of the African art and Egyptian friezes I had studied in art school came back to me. Even now, this craft still makes me feel oddly connected to the primitive artisans who decorated their hand-woven textiles and tools of daily living with similar designs. Like magic, a simple shape, carved by hand, then repeated in succession over yards of fabric becomes a pattern; full of life, imagery, rhythm and color. It is orderly, yet spontaneous—funky, yet surprisingly elegant.

From the first swatch of fabric covered with my original stamped patterns, I was hooked. My ideas began to flow, and I felt energized. Once I figured out how to efficiently print the fabric, I was stamping like mad. I discovered that the method with the least wastage was to cut out the shape I needed for the finished item, leaving generous borders for sewing selvedge. I went to work measuring and cutting out squares for potholders, pillows, tote bags, change purses and other very simple shapes.

I assembled all the supplies I needed—cans of textile inks, fabric, scissors, batting, pillow forms, and stiff brushes for applying the ink to the potato's surface—and of course, bags of potatoes. I started my printmaking experiment in an extra bedroom in the house, but soon realized I would need more space. So I enlisted Steve's help to outfit the upstairs of our barn for my workspace. He constructed a primitive wooden worktable for me that took up almost the whole room and built a small deck and stairs for easy access at the back of the building. He had his carpentry shop on the first floor of the barn, and it was a crazy mess, but it did have all the required tools to make this happen rather quickly. I think he was almost as excited as I to see what might evolve.

The next objective was to find someone to sew for me. Even if I'd had excellent sewing skills (which I didn't), I had far too much to handle to be able to do that too. I asked around a little bit and found a couple of women who were accomplished seamstresses and, as working moms, were happy to have a job they could take home and execute while their children were sleeping. Before long, I was so busy that my piecework occupied all of their free time and gave them a nice extra income.

I remember the very first item they sewed for me. It was a potholder (I wish I still had it!) stamped with a series of blue birds on a tan background with a geometric border printed around the edge. It had the essence of the tribal art I loved but was a three-dimensional functional item that was so beautiful you could hang it on the wall. When I first saw it, I was insanely happy. Who knew a quilted square of cotton fabric stamped with images of egrets could bring me such ridiculous joy? It was as though, in that one moment, holding the potholder in my hand gave me the power to see into the future. I was overcome with creative energy. I wanted to cut potatoes and stamp fabric all day long.

I bought a baby monitor, so I could work while my toddlers were napping. At this point, Erik was in preschool and Brita was still a baby. This gave me small pockets of time to attend to my artwork, and I fit it in whenever possible. It was sporadic, at first, but later, we established a rhythm and then I found daycare. Brita was an easy baby and adjusted well to the series of child-care providers that came to care for her. If it hadn't been for the kids, I would have worked incessantly, so I was grateful they provided a reminder to get out of my studio and play. They grounded me.

By necessity, I became very organized. I knew if I were to let things slide at all, I would never catch up. All of a sudden, the quiet contemplation of my walks in the woods and days alone in my studio had become a distant memory. My daily meditation and yoga practice went out the window. Life had taken on a completely new tempo.

There were days where I felt perched on a knife-edge, just barely able to manage it all. I was captivated by the business, as well as the art. So I embraced the stress, accepting it as my new norm.

My creative drive was so compelling, it was almost unbearable. An inner engine was ignited, and, to this day, it hums pretty much all the time. Thus began a lifelong internal struggle to balance my conflicting needs—that of spiritual equilibrium with my innate creative compulsiveness.

There were a few people and organizations who helped move me towards a more professional approach to business. A group of women friends had started a cooperative show space called *The Center and Main Gallery* in Gloucester and asked me to join. At that point, I wasn't sure I had enough of a body of work to warrant it. My friend Kate, who was a founding member of the gallery, a new mother and an artisan entrepreneur herself, was very encouraging and coerced me into taking the next step to make my experiment into a real enterprise.

She was a potter who had developed a great little business, manufacturing ceramic earrings inspired by traditional Japanese designs. She had a few employees and a busy workshop in a large four-story building her family owned, just off of Main Street in Gloucester. *The Center and Main Gallery* was located on the first floor. Not only did Kate have a thriving livelihood with her ceramic jewelry business, she was also a former teacher who loved to see other people blossom. (Having this kind of moral support is critical for anyone embarking on a new endeavor. I couldn't have achieved what I did without the support of my network of friends who were also trying to make a living from their creativity.)

I had yet to make the leap from artisan to entrepreneur. Kate and I took turns watching each other's kids, and our sons, who were the same age, became best friends. She was like my soul sister and commercial conscience, all wrapped up in one dynamic package. Constantly she would urge me, "Sigrid, you need to get this stuff out there—people are going to love it! You are going to sell like crazy. But you need business cards and a logo and some sort of catalog if you want to consider selling wholesale."

That word "wholesale" alarmed me. "I don't know. I'm happy doing what I'm doing. I don't want to make it too slick," I explained to her. Perhaps it was some residual anti-capitalist belief from my hippie days that prevented me from taking the commercial prospects seriously, but I still felt ambivalent about "selling out." (Ironic—considering where my career ended up later.)

My membership at the gallery was initiated with a show of my new work. Most people had never seen anything quite like the textile prints I made with my potato stamps. A full-sized quilt hung in the window, all hand printed, with blue-hued seascape motifs on unbleached muslin. There were dozens of pillows and a few wall hangings and a basket of potholders. By then, I had added quilted vests and jackets to my repertoire and was pleased that my home-sewers could construct them.

Showing my work in this gallery was my debut. I was now part of the craft community and I felt stronger by the association. I was touched that Kate and the other members of the gallery were so happy to have me there and encouraged my success.

People seemed to genuinely love what I was doing. The excitement that my pieces generated was amazing. I sold more than I ever expected and was so proud to have my parents come and see me in this setting. Even if my life was a little haphazard, trying to balance this budding business with housework and childrearing, it was worth it.

Once I got on track creatively, there was no stopping me. I adored what I was doing and was buoyed by the positive feedback. Why not try to make money doing it? At this point I had cash flowing out—babysitters, supplies, stitchers, membership dues. It was time to raise some revenue, get some cash flowing *in*. So, I revved up my engines and hired an assistant to help me ramp up the textile print production. She helped cut and prepare the fabric pieces and assemble the bundles for the home-sewers. I taught her how to print and that speeded up the process considerably. Despite the fact that she wasn't a working artist, she caught on easily, and it was fun having someone to talk to while we were working.

It remained my job to cut the potatoes. First, I sliced them in half with a sharp paring knife and then used an exacto blade to create the finer detail of the shapes from the flat surface. The natural moisture of the potato blended easily with the water-based ink, which I took care to subtly change every few times the potato was stamped, creating a lovely modulated effect.

I became skilled at positive/negative cognizance, which is a must for a printmaker. The key to this is knowing that every shape stamped onto the fabric is actually printed in reverse. I learned to visualize the print patterns in advance and then cut the potatoes to achieve the shape. For example, fish swim opposite of how they're cut on the potato and birds face backwards. Leaves and flowers are more forgiving, some shapes work in any direction, and so on.

Keeping in mind that, once a potato is cut, it lasts about a half hour, before it begins to shrivel, there is an immediacy to this method of hand-printing. The shape loses its definition quickly, especially if stamped repeatedly. The swiftness of the medium matched my natural tempo, so it wasn't difficult for me to move fast and get even more done in a short amount of time. My style is "if it can't be done fast, then maybe someone else should do it".

I got very good at carving, since I had to cut my signature shapes over and over again, sometimes in the same print session. Every day was the same ritual—cut the fabric, lay it out, cut the stamps, mix the colors, brush ink onto the potato and stamp on the fabric, repeat. After this, the fabric was heat set and bundled into packages with thread, zippers, buttons and batting for the sewers to pick up and take home to sew.

I enjoyed all aspects of the design process, not just the printmaking. I set to work creating a catalog of all the things I made, complete with prices. It was very funky and whimsical, illustrated in pen and ink, with handwritten descriptions. My logo came to me easily—a row of egrets with slender blades of marsh grass inside a geometric border inscribed with the text "Sigrid Olsen Handprints" in graceful type, printed in black on natural card stock. I was beginning to see the company come to life, as though another member of our family was being born. It turned out to be much more work than another baby, however.

I balanced the demands of motherhood with this burgeoning career, still in its infancy. Baby Brita became a fixture at local craft fairs where she sat perched in a straw basket, her bandana-wrapped head peeking out from the baby bunting I made for her. (This item was one of my best sellers—an ingeniously simple design that Steve came up with.)

I was making crib quilts as baby gifts, and one day, I laid Brita down on top of one to verify the size when Steve said he had an idea.

"Why don't you put buttons down the front so you can wrap her up in it? "

I tried it, and her little head disappeared. She was wrapped like a *burrito*.

"Here, try this," he said and turned down each corner exposing her face again. "All you have to do is put a loop on each corner and sew a button down here and you have a great little baby bunting."

It was adorable. The best part was it was easy to undo and open up, so I could lay it flat. That way, wherever we went she had her familiar quilt on which to sit and play. I started making them for sale and gave them away for baby shower gifts. Most of my friends had used them for their own children. I know they became favorite bedtime companions because I saw how worn out they were after years of being dragged around everywhere and never retired. More than one was so far gone after hundreds of washings that it had to be stitched into a tiny pillow to keep it intact after it had turned to rags following years of faithful use.

As I became immersed in *Sigrid Olsen Hand Prints*, I realized I had an aptitude for the practical as well as the creative aspects. I enjoyed problem solving, figuring prices, setting up systems and planning for the future. All my creative energy went into the business—designing and printing the fabric as well as managing the production as well as the marketing and sales of the finished product through the few outlets I had. My favorites were the craft fairs, which I attended in locations all over New England. I loved setting up the table with my wares and watching people's reactions first hand. It was quite busy, especially during the Holidays, and the fees were so low, it was well worth it, both financially and personally.

Joining a local craft's cooperative called *Cape Ann Artisans* led to the next big step. This community was the ideal place for me to launch a business. I was never intimidated or forced to grow faster than was comfortable. Cape Ann is small and rather intimate, with a vibrant summer tourist trade, enabling start-ups like mine to take root and blossom without high rents and fierce competition. It didn't take long for word to spread about my funky, original designs and, before long, I had a decent client list. The positive response helped fuel my desire to keep going, building on my small success.

A few members of the artisan group decided to pool our resources and rent a gallery in the tourist area of Rockport, the town where I lived. We called it *Ten Hands*, an apt name referring to the five of us (and our hands) who founded it. We shared the responsibility for everything—rent, set-up, display, inventory, and sales. For me, it provided a wonderful window into the workings of a small tourist town and boosted my confidence, because my things began to sell very well. It was great payback with little investment or risk and was the perfect outlet for a working mother with little business expertise.

Since we were all at the same level of volume, the group of us got along well and keeping the books was simple. We collected the revenue from our individual sales at the end of the month and shared the expenses equally. I had a slight advantage because I had help making my products, where the jewelers, weaver and potters I shared with had to make each item by hand on their own. This enabled me to keep my volume high and my prices low, increasing my sales significantly.

Although my work was moving more quickly, the others remained caring and supportive, knowing that this new enterprise was important to me. Instead of competing, we encouraged one another. The sense of empowerment I gained from being connected to other entrepreneurs is what sustained me when the hours were long, the work was overwhelming, and money was tight.

The passion I brought to my little enterprise came from somewhere deep inside me and bubbled up effortlessly as I took each step along the way. (It is the same energy that fuels me today.) Just as I was settling into the rhythm of my life as mother, wife and entrepreneur, the most incredible and life-changing moment was about to happen.

Fashioning a Career

*"I have been impressed with the urgency of doing.
Knowing is not enough, we must apply.
Being willing is not enough, we must do."*
—Leonardo da Vinci

I was fully engaged in building the *Sigrid Olsen Handprints* business and raising my family when one day in 1984 a man named Peter Wagner came into my Rockport shop and inadvertently changed my life completely. I wasn't looking to expand much further than this small gallery and the few craft shows I attended to sell my work. I was busy and quite happy for the time being.

When Peter showed up and started asking questions about my prints, I didn't think much of it. He was an older gentleman (fifty-three to my thirty-one) dressed in preppy khaki shorts and a polo shirt. I wasn't sure how he would relate to the unpolished craftiness of my work, but he was definitely interested, taking note especially of the blouses, tees and vests that were adorned with my signature birds, fish and seascapes. He complimented me on their originality and was curious how they were produced. I explained the mechanics of my little cottage industry and when he inquired, "So, how many of these can you make in a day?" I replied,

"Maybe a dozen or so." His face registered a moment of puzzlement, but he persisted, still intrigued by something.

Then he started talking more animatedly, "I just got home from a trip to Maui and I think that prints are going to be the next big trend. Ever heard of a company called *Jams*? They are those long shorts with wild tropical prints that surfers wear but now everyone's wearing them. I could see your prints on shorts like *Jams*. I've been in this business a long time, and I have a nose for spotting trends. I think these could be pretty special. Then there is this other line from Hawaii called *Reynspooner*. Have you seen it? They print on cotton but then make the garments from the back of the fabric. It's different, unique. Your prints are not just good. They are great. Just great."

He was all wound up and began speaking at a pace that I couldn't quite follow, jumping from topic to topic with reckless enthusiasm. I was lost. In years to come, I would learn to navigate the currents of his uncharted conversations and be able to extract the important points and then develop a plan of action from his ramblings. His haphazard exuberance fueled everything we accomplished together, but my skill at translating his lively monologues was what enabled us to harness his energy and make it work. However, that day, I had not yet honed that particular talent. I listened, intimidated by his apparent affluence and his conservative appearance. He went on to impart bits of wisdom he had gleaned from thirty years selling apparel, quite successfully it seemed.

"My trip to Hawaii was a sales award from my company. I was top salesman this year. Did more business than anyone else in the U.S. Just selling here in New England. I grew up in New Jersey, but we summered in Annisquam. Now I live just up the street, right here in Rockport. We have a great little house, overlooks Sandy Bay."

He clearly had done well for himself selling apparel. I felt like he was listing his accomplishments for me like a resume. I was impressed, but also somewhat shy to show my handprints in this context. He was more charming than condescending, however. I think he genuinely saw the beauty in my work and was amused by my artsy appearance. I was sure he had no idea how primitive my operation really was.

"I'd like to talk to you about this some more, throw some ideas around. Why don't you come over to my house next week, and we'll see what we can come up with. What do you say? Okay with you?"

I was shell-shocked. His banter was like machine gun fire and I was having trouble keeping up. One of my strengths (which I've counted on throughout my entire career) is an ability to think on my feet. I retained my composure, looked him straight in the eye and said, "Sure. I'd like that. See you on Tuesday morning. I can be there by 9:30 after I get the kids off to school and day care." Just like that. It wasn't like offers like this were an everyday occurrence. When he walked out, I had a strange sense of excitement and anticipation, but I never expected anything close to what happened.

When the day came for our meeting, I packed some sketches and fabrics into a bag and hopped on my bike for the short ride to his house. When I got there, I was dazzled by the openness of the space and the incredible view. After a brief tour, we sat at his dining room table and mapped out a plan. I was learning as we went along—I knew nothing about business, beyond what I had stumbled upon through my own experimentation. Handprints, home-sewers, craft fairs and artisan tours were the extent of my knowledge. However, my instincts told me I would figure it out, so I wanted to keep exploring this idea. I had faith we could do more with my prints than I had ever imagined. Instead of being terrified by the unknown, I was stimulated by the challenge. I felt the protection of my guardian angel guiding me towards my destiny.

There was very little time to worry about how I would fare on this new path, because there were practical problems to surmount. The first problem we had to solve was how to produce yards of fabric to make multiples of each item. I had been printing one thing at a time and that clearly wasn't going to work anymore. Peter's qualifications were in the area of sales and merchandising, not manufacturing. So we were both feeling our way.

This was in the days before Google—before personal computers, smart phones and even fax machines—so our research was done primarily by word of mouth. One call would lead us to another resource and so on. Peter had no fear of making phone calls, talking to each person as if he'd known them for years. After a few calls, he located a silkscreen textile printer in Western Massachusetts and set up an appointment to view the facilities so we could have a chat.

That week, we made the three-hour drive west to meet with them. I was fascinated by every aspect of the print facility and asked a million questions. The fabrics were beautiful, very upscale. It dawned on me when I went there how insular my life had become—there was a big world out there with people doing miraculous, creative things. Things I had always wanted to do but never had the opportunity to take the leap and explore.

I still struggle with that itchiness to learn more, experience more, see more, even though I also know that finding inner peace is about being happy with what you've got, satisfied with where you are. This internal tug-of-war is my personal quandary, the conflict of my contrasting personality traits.

Being in this fabric facility heightened my creative urges. The proximity to all the colors and patterns electrified my senses and reinforced my belief that this type of work would figure prominently in my future. After a brief exchange, however, I was disappointed to learn that their specialty was in the field of interior design and upholstery fabrics, not the lighter weight cottons we would use for apparel. Luckily, they knew someone in upstate New York they thought would be perfect for our project. I diligently noted all the details in my notebook, and we returned to Rockport with a plan to visit the other factory as soon as possible. Fortunately, Peter was just as impatient as I, and we were both ready to get this show on the road.

The next task to be handled was to organize the prints. According to Peter, there was a method to determine how they would show best. We chose three or four of our favorite simple patterns that could be easily reproduced by silkscreen and offered each of them in a few different color combinations. We created a chart of sorts to keep track of the different prints and assigned the styles for each one. This was my first lesson in merchandising a fashion collection in its most rudimentary stage of development. We focused on both men's and women's designs in very simple styles, guided by the surf and resort wear that had inspired Peter in Hawaii.

There was never a lack of input. Peter incessantly offered ideas, sketched out on paper napkins, or magazine tear sheets, articles, and notes from news stories that influenced him. Every time we met, he would present a manila folder filled with various scraps of inspiration, thrusting them at me, one after the other. I learned quickly how to sort through the barrage of suggestions and select those that could be put to use. For the most part, though, I was grateful he had plenty of ideas and the enthusiasm to propel this venture forward. Whenever I felt stuck, he would come along with his manic energy and move things along.

I felt awkward having him come to my studio, which he did on a number of occasions to work with me on the prints and colors for the line. He had to pick his way through tools and other detritus that littered our yard and climb the rickety steps to the makeshift studio I had devised in the upstairs of our barn. In my workshop, there were bags of potatoes, piles of fabric and trims, bundles waiting to be picked up by home-sewers and stacks of books, magazines, sketches and prints everywhere.

His house was pristine, in comparison, and I knew he was very orderly by nature. I was embarrassed for him to see my state of disarray. However, the chaos didn't seem to faze him as much as I feared. He concentrated on the artwork and ignored the clutter, making comments and suggestions until we were both satisfied with the look of the prints for our line. I think there was something about the mess that signaled authenticity to him, and he accepted it as part of my creative process.

It didn't take me long to understand how a clean, uncluttered workspace would help me. Reclaiming my territory from the mish-mash of materials gave me a sense of accomplishment and provided a clean slate from which to work. Once I tackled the disorder, I felt calmer, even in the face of pressing deadlines and numerous works-in-progress.

Peter and I didn't spend that much time together in my studio, though. Most of our meetings were held at his place at the table, overlooking the sea. I tried hard not to be distracted by the outrageous display of beauty outside the window. There were sea birds and sailboats against a backdrop of glittering water, and I was mesmerized. With all my artwork spread out on the table, we realized the scene outside the window was reflected in the patterns on the fabric in front of us. Graceful sea birds, egrets, wave patterns and fish comprised the collection of prints emanating effortlessly from my hand.

One morning, Peter greeted me with the announcement that he had an idea for the name of our new company. He loved to build suspense and began talking at length about the importance of the sea birds to the feel of our brand and mentioned the fact that the egret in particular had been the symbol of my hand print business from the start.

"Are you ready?" he asked.

"I guess so," I said apprehensively. This was an important step and I was wary about letting him take the lead on this one.

"I thought about your birds, you know, the ones on your business card. The egrets. And then your name, of course, has to be in it somehow. So, I came up with *Segrets*. But not just that...*Segrets Sun Prints*, because of your prints as well as the fact that we are both inspired by the beach and resort life style. *Segrets Sun Prints*. What do you think? Great huh?" He gave me a broad smile and looked at me expectantly.

What could I say? At first, I was unimpressed, not crazy about the play on words. I also felt cursed by my unusual name throughout my childhood and suffered frequent mispronunciations, not to mention the silly nicknames I had endured in elementary school—seaweed, cigar, cigarette. But I didn't have a better idea, so I agreed. Hence, *Segrets Sun Prints* was born. (Years later, we changed from *Segrets Sun Prints* to SIGRID OLSEN for the label, but *Segrets, Inc.* remained the corporate name for many years.)

OK...so we had a name...but we did not yet have a line of samples to show a buyer. Time was passing quickly, and we had already missed the first window for the Spring 1985 selling season. Without realizing it, I was thrust into the fast pace of the fashion timetable. I learned that for a line to be sold in stores for Spring, the samples had to be ready by August of the year before. Sample prep time was at least four months and design time another three, so essentially, we were working nine months to a year in advance. Gestation time for a baby and a fashion collection is about the same.

We decided we would aim our launch for Summer 1985 and designed the collection accordingly, knowing it was a smaller season and not the ideal time to present a new line. But because our entire look was resort-driven, we couldn't launch for Fall, and we didn't want to wait another full year. We were still on schedule for the summer release, but we had to hurry.

Our next step was to get the fabric printed, so we set off for the long drive to upstate New York to visit the silkscreen factory that had been recommended. We had sent the designs ahead of time, so they could create the screens that would be used to print the yardage.

I had never been inside a factory like this before and the scale was amazing. Buckets of inks lined the walls, and the tables were the longest I had ever seen. We were welcomed by Charles, the owner, an ebullient man about my age, who gave us a tour of the facilities while chatting about his artistic background and asking questions about mine. I felt comfortable right away and was excited about what we could do together. (This feeling of hyped-up anticipation was one that would become very familiar to me as my career progressed, especially when I was presented with opportunities to see my designs come to life in different media.)

We were invited into his office to see the small strike-offs he had prepared, and he warned me the color matching was less than ideal. My heart sank a little when I saw them—the hues were way off, either too bright or too dull—the subtlety of my carefully blended color schemes completely lost. He admitted that color matching was not his strength, and he could use a little help. I tried to describe verbally what was needed, "add a touch of blue and lots of yellow," for example, but felt hampered by the indirect method of communication. I think Charles could sense my artistic frustration and offered:

"Sigrid, want to don an apron and try mixing them yourself?"

"Sure!" I said, without hesitation, and followed him into the color mixing area. This unreserved confidence was my way of tackling most obstacles. I had faith in what I knew and was comfortable just plunging in.

In my studio, my method of color mixing for potato prints was to spoon the inks into an egg carton by eye. A scoop of this, a dash of that, and I was ready to go. This was a whole new ballgame. They used huge industrial blenders with at least a five-gallon capacity. Unfazed, I began to create my color palette, measuring inks as I poured them into the vats, so they would be able to reproduce the formula in the future. I laughed to myself as I combined these enormous quantities of pigment, thinking how I never would have pictured this scene in all my years of creating crafts by hand. But I loved it. Every ink-splashed, smudge-filled moment. In a short time, we had perfected the custom blends and the technicians set to work printing the fabric.

I watched in awe as yards of my printed egrets and fish appeared before my eyes. In the time it would have taken me to lay out a table of a dozen square pillows, cut the potatoes, mix the inks and stamp them onto the fabric, they had completed fifty yards, enough to make an entire set of samples.

There were four different patterns, each available in three colors, so it would be a day or two before they would complete the whole collection. The printed cotton was so beautiful to me, I insisted on taking small cuttings to hold and admire all the way home, caressing them like a new baby. When the rest was finished, it was rolled onto bolts and shipped to the garment factory we had located in Worcester to sew our samples.

I couldn't believe this was all really happening. In the weeks I'd spent getting to know Peter and learning about the apparel business, I never abandoned my commitment to Sigrid Olsen Handprints. His ideas always seemed compelling, but a little farfetched to me. I decided not to get my hopes up and to stay true to myself. I still worked in my studio with my potato prints and participated in the Ten Hands Gallery and various craft shows, all the while balancing this with time at home with my family. Even though I had faith in myself, I had no idea where it would all lead, and I did not indulge myself in extravagant dreams. Not yet.

The first Segrets Sun Prints collection was very simple. Shorts, blouses, camp shirts and tees in a dozen or so print color-ways. We used basic cotton sheeting in two qualities, a lighter weight for tops (shirts and blouses) and one for bottoms. The fabric was hand screened in beautiful shades of blue, teal, aqua, lime, pinks and corals.

The prints were so distinctive and looked great together, so Peter devised a unique method of showing them to buyers. He invented a clever sales tool he called a "swatch roll"—patchwork squares of prints arranged into one long strip of fabric backed by unbleached muslin and padded like a quilt. This long narrow quilt was then rolled up and secured with cotton ties for transporting and packing with the samples. We had one of my home sewers stitch a number of them to provide to the sales team we hadn't even hired yet. When Peter saw the finished product he was delighted, jumping up and down with excitement. He demonstrated over and over the "unveiling" of the prints by unfastening the ties and rolling it out on the table with a dramatic snap of the wrist. All our colorful prints were displayed at once. The impact was quite irresistible.

At this point, we were almost out of money. I had none to begin with, and Peter had invested to the extent he was able. At least we had a number of samples we could show to prospective investors, which we did as soon as we could. The Fashion and Boutique Show was scheduled that month in New York and Peter knew a number of companies and individuals who would be attending, so we went to see what kind of interest we could prompt with our groovy swatch roll and small sample line.

To be among industry giants with my little collection of prints was incredibly humbling. I felt shy, but Peter forged ahead, accustomed to generating excitement in any circumstance from his decades in sales. We spent an exhausting day walking the aisles in search of a benefactor with no luck. This was exactly why I hadn't wanted to get my hopes up. All the work we had done, the planning, the research, the money invested would be wasted if we couldn't find someone to believe in our venture. By evening, we hadn't accomplished much and were feeling somewhat discouraged when we parted ways for the night. I headed to my grandmother's apartment on Thirty-Seventh Street, and he went to his hotel.

After dinner, just as I was preparing to go to sleep, the phone rang. It was Peter. He was very animated. I wondered if he had been drinking.

"Sig. Do you believe in miracles?"

Hmmm, I thought. What's he up to now?

"Only if they're good," I replied, skeptical.

He laughed. "Well, I think this is a good one."

He proceeded to recount his evening for me on the phone. He had stopped into a small Italian restaurant for dinner near his hotel. He happened to notice a young, well-dressed man at a nearby table reading a book about investing, so he struck up a conversation with him. Peter always did this anywhere we went, with waitresses, salespeople, anyone. So, this didn't surprise me. What did surprise me is that it worked. The man's name was David, and he was a venture capitalist, who managed his family's nine-figure portfolio and made smaller investments on his own.

This captured Peter's attention. "Oh really? So what kind of stuff do you invest in?"

David, who was very mild-mannered in comparison to Peter, replied: "Oh, all sorts of things—Off-Broadway, retail, technology, some fashion." I could imagine Peter's eyes lighting up at this.

There was his opening, and he jumped right in. "Well, I just happen to have a little company you might want to invest in. Why don't you come to my hotel tomorrow, and I can show you samples so you can decide for yourself." David agreed and they made a plan for the next morning at 11 o'clock.

I drifted off to sleep that night in a state of anxious anticipation, not knowing what to expect from their meeting the next day. I was beginning to feel a buoyant atmosphere of good fortune surround me, and I wasn't disappointed. It turned out that David was very taken with the whole package Peter presented and wrote a check on the spot, impressed by the urgency of the fashion calendar no doubt. His financial support turned out to fuel our growth for the next fifteen years, and he was very much a part of our success.

Peter and David bonded right away, sharing their parallel personal histories (Peter was a Dartmouth grad and David had a law degree from Harvard), undoubtedly enjoying the ways in which they differed as much as their similarities. Peter's outgoing and audacious salesmanship was a clear contrast to David's quiet intellectualism. I think David found Peter refreshing and Peter always respected David's intelligence and refined upbringing.

My world was expanding way beyond the small town of Rockport and the safe circle of friends and family who had nurtured me since my college years. I had two small children, a husband and now a blossoming career in its infancy. I already had the sense that I was caught between two worlds. I tried very hard to stay grounded and free to dream at the same time. It was uplifting to receive encouragement from people like Peter and David and the few other professionals I had met during our research phase.

Still, there was so much I had yet to discover. I was eager to learn, yet cautious about losing touch with myself in the process. This desire to hold true to my core values is something I have wrestled with throughout my career, and only now have found a way of life that allows me to integrate them into everything I do. But during my thirties, it was a time of exploration and discovery, of striving and accomplishment. These things were important to me as I climbed the ladder of success. By the time I was forty, I arrived at a new plateau, and yet, I still strove for more.

The process of building a company unfolded naturally. We worked hard and tried to go as far as we could with our combined talents. But after a short time, it was clear that Peter and I were in way over our heads when it came to sourcing and production. There were so many details to consider and so many things that could go wrong.

We began our search for a manufacturing manager right away. Luckily, Peter knew a few people in the business and, before long, we were directed to a woman with several years of experience in apparel production, almost all of which was located in Hong Kong. She convinced us we could produce the whole line in Asia at a workable price and with considerably less margin for error. It was a huge leap to move from stamping inches of fabric with potato prints to manufacturing garments halfway around the world, and it was all happening very fast.

My first trip to Hong Kong occurred that year, and I stayed two weeks. Once it was decided that I would have to go to Asia and oversee the prints, I was nervous. It would be the first time away from my children for any length of time. I sensed (correctly) that this would be a turning point for my career and my life and I wasn't sure how we would all fare. When I mentioned my apprehension to my husband, he answered, "Well, then don't go." Clearly, he didn't understand I was just airing my anxiety, but I really had to do this. Or maybe he sensed that it foretold a change to our simple family life.

It was then I realized I really wanted to go. Staying home, missing this opportunity, was not an option. It was as though boarding that 747 and traversing the globe was the first in a number of flights towards a new life—one that would eventually take me away from my marriage and send me into the orbit of a much wider world.

I had a lot to learn about the apparel industry. Our trading company in Hong Kong was a small office that gave our startup business all the care and attention it needed. I happily absorbed every bit of technical information that came at me every day—mastering the art of creating flat sketches and spec sheets, approving color swatches, prints and lab dips, measuring samples as they arrived from each factory.

That first trip to Hong Kong introduced me to even larger factories than I had visited at home. The silkscreen tables were longer and more plentiful, and the work was done very quickly, yet there was a primitive aspect to the facilities. Barely air-conditioned, the men who operated the silk screens, moving them systematically down each table to print the yardage, were shirtless and scantily clad in shorts or loin cloths to stay cool in the steamy workspace. Long bamboo poles above each table held the billowing cloth overhead to help it air dry after it was printed. I spent hours at this factory working closely with the printers to get the right colors and select the strike-offs that would make it into production. I got to know them and thanked them all profusely for indulging me in repeated trials of color combinations until we got it right. (Nowadays, we fine-tune all the prints by computer design before they are even submitted to the factory, so this kind of impromptu collaboration is unheard of.)

I still couldn't believe my good fortune to have all this technology at my disposal. Seeing my handprint designs in massive quantities was overwhelming and humbling. To make this many garments, we would have to find people to buy them all. That was Peter's job, and, back at home he was hard at work doing just that. With his signature gusto, he was able to entice sales reps he knew to take on a new line. He was passionate and convincing as only Peter could be. Fortunately, his enthusiasm was contagious, and he created a fervor that helped propel us into the mainstream of specialty retail.

The only problem was that his unrestrained zeal caused him to order enough inventory to last us for the next three years. That first collection was a big hit, but we were way overstocked and learned a bitter lesson about sales projections from this overestimation. We survived that first misstep and proceeded to create collections that had a fresh, natural appeal for the next several years.

The foundation of *Segrets Sun Prints* was strong because it was composed of hundreds of small specialty stores all across America that carried the line. How did we achieve this? Peter's experience had taught him that the best way to capture this myriad buying entity was to reach them where they live. Literally.

In less than two years, he was able to assemble a nationwide team of sales reps, covering every part of the country. He was a sales rep himself, so he knew very well how it worked. Swatch roll in hand, he visited all the major markets—New England, New York, Dallas, California, Chicago, Denver, Atlanta, Florida and even the Caribbean—spreading the gospel of *Segrets Sun Prints*.

Many of the reps that were hired those first two years stayed with the company until the bitter end. And it *was* bitter at the end—just like me, they thought they would be with *Segrets* forever, never expecting the turn of events that brought our collaboration to a close, less than two decades after it began. Their loyalty was a reflection, not just of the amazing success they achieved, but of the human bond we established over the years we worked together.

Because we were breaking new ground, we were open to anything. One of our first rep teams was a couple who lived and traveled with the collection on a sailboat selling the line to stores on remote islands in the British Virgin Islands and West Indies. I had friends who called me after their island vacations, shocked that they saw my clothing in some remote corner of the Caribbean. All up and down the eastern seaboard, the *Segrets* label could be spotted in unexpected locales like bait and tackle shops, marine provisioners and yacht clubs, all of whom loved the casual, sea-themed look of the line.

On the West Coast, in Vermont and Colorado, some of our best accounts were ski shops and outdoor stores, which expanded our reach beyond the traditional sportswear stores ordinarily targeted for this type of clothing. The reps were meeting with approval in every venue, and they blanketed their territories with our product.

The orders were small, but consistent, and the reorders were very good. This kind of solid base helped us grow a strong and stable business. The creativity of our designs and the personal attention we gave our customers made all the long days and nights of labor fun.

At home in Rockport, my kids were getting used to sharing me with the business. We had a modest, but light-filled office above a convenience store downtown, and they were able to walk there after school to see me (and get money for snacks). They wore child-sized versions of our printed styles when we had a kids' line and even modeled for our catalog. They got to know the office staff by name and had the secure knowledge of where I was and what I was doing when I wasn't at home.

However, it wasn't ideal. I missed so much. Consumed by my workload and devoted to the growth of my company, I wasn't fully there even when I thought I was. While the other mothers in our small town attended every PTA meeting and sports event, I was tending to my business.

At one point I decided I would join them—do my part to participate in my children's education. The first (and only) parent's meeting I attended was focused on an upcoming fundraiser they were planning. There was a lively discussion debating the merits of pancakes versus spaghetti with passionate arguments from all sides.

Once the menu was decided and other details secured, it was time for the big question—what shall we do with the money we raise? I had been lulled into a boredom-induced, half-sleep until now and at this point I sat up in disbelief. They had just spent the majority of the evening arguing about how to raise the most money, but never had discussed why. It seemed a bit backwards to me. More discussion ensued, and I honestly can't remember what was decided. What I do remember is that when all the discourse died down I raised my hand—" I know I am new to this, but I thought that we would be discussing our children's education and talking about curriculum and that sort of thing. Is that something that we will do another time?" I was met with puzzled stares. They looked at one another and finally declared, "Mmm, yeah, that's a good idea..."

That was my last PTA meeting. I was far too busy to take another night away from home for this, and I didn't see how this would benefit my kids either.

Over the years, I have attended hundreds, probably thousands, of meetings between my work, and various boards and committees I've joined, and never came to appreciate them. They usually seem like a waste of time. My impatience often made the lengthy discussions intolerable. I became known as the feisty one who always got right to the point, asking the questions no one else dared to ask. I would always rather be *doing* than talking about it.

My life became more and more divided. I was one person at the office—focused, productive and organized—and another at home—distracted, stressed and disorganized. When I contrasted the two situations, it was a revelation. At the office, people were self-motivated, obedient—they did whatever I asked them to do.

Not so at home. It was a normal household with active children, a working husband, unfinished projects all over the house and the usual mountain of household tasks to tackle every day. In comparison to my workplace, it was chaos.

I was a woman with two jobs, not that uncommon a situation for much of the population. Every working parent knows the drill. You wake early, get the kids ready for school, collect the books and papers, make lunch, rushing all the time. Then, an eight-hour work-day followed by a full evening as cook, cleaner and homework police. After a brief sleep, you do it again, all with the nagging feeling you are not doing anything that well at all.

Eventually, the new person I was becoming, and the vastness of my experiences, distanced me from my husband, and we grew apart. It was a heart-wrenching process to move out on my own, but my instincts told me it was time. I was so young when we married, barely out of my teens. I felt I had to establish who I was and move forward at my own pace. Steve and I have always been friends and always will be, so our mutual respect and concern for the children kept the split amicable. But it wasn't easy for any of us, particularly the kids.

When I became a single parent, staying balanced was even harder, except for the fact that my obligations were reduced from three to two...work and childrearing. The relationship no longer required attention. On days the kids were with their father, I had more freedom, but it was lonely. I felt thrust back to my childhood, the empty rooms echoing the vacancy in my heart. (Loneliness is a condition that I fought for many years until I learned to use the time to turn inward and find peace. I wish I had learned that sooner.)

I spent too much time working and not enough seeking refuge from the manic lifestyle that consumed me.

The excitement of creating a business was an antidote for any hardships in my personal life. There were many times I found solace from problems by immersion in my work.

As more people joined the team, a feeling of camaraderie was growing. We were working together and achieving great things. I think my lack of previous business experience was actually a benefit in this case, generating a constant sense that we were breaking new ground and weren't tied to any old patterns or established ways of doing things. It was a true entrepreneurial venture. The spirit of innovation permeated everything, even the most mundane financial and administrative duties. It was a heady time, and those who were part of it recall it as one of the highlights of their career.

In the late eighties, another important person entered the scene at Segrets. She became my close collaborator for the next eighteen years. We were just beginning to design sweaters to include in our collections and quickly realized we needed help. As often happens in the fashion business, our CFO had worked with someone at a previous job who he thought could assist us, so he gave her a call. While I was relatively new to the industry, Dorian, the knitwear designer, had years of rigorous training during her time working for Mast Industries, which was a local production arm for The Limited Stores. She was a star there, having created the top-selling shaker knit sweaters that had a very long and lucrative run at The Limited in the eighties. Even I had a few in my closet.

She and I instantly connected. Both viewed ourselves as artists first and loved the blending of creativity and commerce. I have never met another designer who shares my unusual balance of artistic and operational expertise. This helped our business in ways I cannot measure.

When she arrived the day of her interview (though she claims she was just there as a consultant and never expected a job offer), we immediately found common ground. After a few minutes of conversation, we discovered many shared experiences. Both single moms, we compared notes: "When did you separate?"

"Just last year."

"Me too!"

"How many kids do you have?"

"Two…older boy and younger girl…"

"Me too!"

She smiled. We did a high five and that was it. We knew we would find a way to work together.

Dorian was just as driven as I was. She admired my quick learning style and I was humbled by her vast experience and skill. I was also amazed to see how she managed to balance her family and work with remarkable success. Over the next few years, I had a crash course in knitwear and applied my distinctive color and print designs to the hand knit sweaters we created together. We literally designed them from scratch, sketching out the patterns full size on drawing paper and sending it overseas to be stitched into the colorful cardigans and tunics that established us as leaders in our market.

We often traveled to Asia together, sometimes alone and sometimes with a team of designers and product managers. The goal there was to get as many samples approved as we could in the shortest time, so we spent long nights in my suite at the Regent Hotel after traveling all day to visit factories and work with our agents in the office. The jet lag is brutal to begin with. Hong Kong is twelve hours ahead, so sleep is elusive. But we took advantage of our sleeplessness to continue working on the samples that arrived daily from the factories. Bleary-eyed, we would line them up for scrutiny and decide which we liked, which we didn't, which needed improvement and what was missing.

I remember one particular night. It was probably two o'clock in the morning and we were sitting, more accurately, lounging on the couch or draped on pillows on the floor, just staring at a lineup of sweaters as though we were watching TV. We were silent for the longest time. Once we realized what we were doing it seemed so absurd we just burst out laughing and decided maybe it was time to go to bed. After sixteen hours of concentrating, you reach a point of diminishing returns.

This kind of intimacy in the workplace meant so much to me then and still does. I like relating to others as human beings, understanding their passions, ambitions, frustrations and disappointments. It creates a multidimensional experience that resonates for me and makes the long hours bearable. No matter how busy we were, the quiet diligence of our office was often pierced by peals of laughter. We all worked incredibly hard but knew that the most important thing was to enjoy ourselves.

Every enterprise, if successful, grows in stages. We had risen to the top of our game at this level of business with joy and were about to take another leap.

~ 108 ~

Becoming Sigrid Olsen

"We are what we pretend to be.
So we must be careful what we pretend to be."
—Kurt Vonnegut

Segrets Sun Prints was a diamond in the rough about to get a major polish.

It was 1990, and we had just undergone our first official market research project. It was my initiation into the one-way mirror, consumer focus group scenario, and it was bizarre. These things are like bad reality shows where the people are less elegant, telegenic and sophisticated than Central Casting would ever allow.

I took my seat in a sealed room behind a wall of glass to observe our focus group. We had hired a brand consultant, whose name was (I'm not making this up) *Mr. Brand.* Our goal was to learn how we fared against our competition and how the average consumer felt about the line. Once questioned, it was apparent that most had never heard of *Sigrid Olsen* or *Segrets Sun Prints*, but they fit the loose demographic requirement—age, education, and income. I am guessing the primary determining factor was a willingness to participate.

I felt my anxiety rise as I watched them discuss my line. Uncomfortable as I was, it was fascinating to secretly witness complete strangers talking about me and my company. There was the usual introductory question and answer period, and then Mr. Brand brought out a rack of clothes. He held up various garments of ours as well as our competition, one of which, coincidentally, was *Liz Claiborne*. This was years before we ever dreamed of being part of that entity. It was like a blind taste test. The audience chattered on about what they liked or didn't like with no restraint. They didn't like much.

I realized that my discomfort was intensified by the fact that, for the most part, I agreed. Taken out of context, the clothes looked ordinary, unremarkable, or worse, contrived. Looking on objectively I felt just as critical envisioning a dozen ways that I could improve on what I was seeing. I itched to return to the studio and get back to work. I was used to this.

Designing clothing season after season becomes a faultfinding mission, where all we do is analyze what we have created with ruthless scrutiny. You can never rest on your laurels. There is always room for improvement. I was learning to become hypercritical. I had to fine-tune my eyes to see beyond the fabric and colors before me and attempt to predict what styles would sell and which wouldn't.

But as it turned out, it wasn't the clothes that these ladies wanted to change.

The focus group project produced only one memorable conclusion: the name *Segrets* was not well received. Justifiably, there were complaints that it reminded them of *Victoria's Secret*, as well as comments that the label had the misfortune of rhyming with "regrets" or, worse, sounded like "cigarettes."

Ha! I knew it! I would never escape the curse of my childhood name shame. Here is how I remember the pivotal moment that happened next:

> Ladies: "So, who designs this line anyway?"
> Mr. Brand: "The designer's name is Sigrid
> Olsen. Want to meet her?"
>
> Ladies: "She's here? Sure, we'd love to!"
>
> Mr. Brand: "Sigrid, would you please come out
> here?"
>
> Sigrid: Inwardly cringing, "OK."
>
> Animated conversation ensues.
>
> Ladies: "She seems like such a nice person,
> pretty, too. Why don't you just name the line
> after her?"

And there you have it…the story behind how I unwittingly gave my name to the brand, via Mr. Brand. (I didn't realize at the time that this action would cause me to struggle with my own identity in the future.)

When I returned home to my design team and announced the changes that were about to occur, I felt a little sheepish that my name was now to be front and center, since I had always thought of my work as a group effort. It wasn't such a big deal; most of us didn't like the name *Segrets* anyway. Everyone seemed to accept this as the way of fashion and already looked to me as the leader of our enterprise.

I was now a bona fide designer, and the line began to reflect that. As we grew, I began to concentrate more and more on what I did best—the artistic and conceptual: choosing colors, selecting, designing and editing prints, and art-directing the brand image for our ad campaigns and print media. At this point, I wisely left the other details to the experts.

There was a huge group assigned to production and sourcing, financial planners, sales executives, and then people to manage those people. The larger the line became, the more staff was required to manage it all. Sometimes I would just sit and ponder the complexity and imagine the number of people who touched a garment before it was in the hands of the one who would ultimately wear it.

After less than ten years we had built our own creative community, and it felt like a family. We celebrated each and every person's birthday with a surprise lunch in the conference room, cake, cards and sometimes even gave presents. Even as our numbers kept growing, we remained dedicated to this tradition. Soon though, it felt like we had a birthday party every other day and it started to interfere with our work. Reluctant to let go of this custom, perhaps in fear that this would signal a new, cold depersonalization process, we kept it going as long as we could, even after we made a blanket decision to group all birthdays by month. From time to time, you could still see small gatherings in each department. It didn't matter. This was probably the most conscientious, hardest working bunch in the industry. We always got it done, through the pure force of collective determination. I was astonished at how well it held together even under pressure, yet we still had fun.

Even though my original partner Peter had removed himself from the day-to-day operations, he came to the office almost every day, and he and I were still close. He was just as energetic as ever, and I was forced to lock myself away, behind closed doors, just to be able to get my work done. His continual flow of suggestions was like a relentless idea factory, overwhelming me when I was under a deadline. Before I had one thing finished, there were three more lined up to do. Sometimes, I just wanted to scream, "Stop! I can't add another thing!"

Fortunately, Dorian and I were a high-functioning duo and approached the development of the line with equal creative intensity and dedication while we both managed single motherhood at home. Everywhere we went, everything we saw, fed the concepts we were working on for the coming season. I loved working with her.

We would often call each other at home, even in the midst of tending to our kids, to share a thought or idea that came to us in our off hours. It came to the point it was hard to define what "off hours" were. We were working in our heads all the time. Like a well-trained army on a mission, we had an extraordinary feeling of camaraderie even as we added more people to our team. The way we cooperated and supported one another is highly unusual in this business.

The work was demanding, but sales were soaring, and we loved coming to work every day. *We were rockin' it.*

As a team, we were pioneering a new way of working together—positive, supportive and life affirming. While I loved the creative challenge, I realized the interpersonal was (and is) more important to me than anything else. I took pride in what we had built and was emotionally attached to the people who contributed to our success over the years. I was deeply invested in cultivating the innate talents of my staff, encouraged as I saw them rise to their full potential. It was gratifying to see the pleasure they got from their jobs. By contrast, it was even more distressing when so many started hating it, because they could see everything changing.

Companies, like seasons, have their cycles. By the mid-nineties we had reached a point where our design-by-committee approach wasn't working so well anymore. The business had grown larger and we were in need of fresh leadership. Peter had taken a back seat, and David was only involved when it came to banking or high level financial issues. I felt the full weight of leading the team, and it had become a burden, on top of all the other things I had to do. There was so much more I had to learn, and I needed a new mentor.

Just in time, David and Peter brought in a new President with an impressive resume. Edward M. Jones III (aka EMJIII) was a high-powered fashion veteran with a soft Texas twang. He had presided at several companies, the most notable of which were Calvin Klein, Esprit and Perry Ellis. It was a little intimidating for me, a self-made entrepreneur, new to the glamorous world of fashion. I was astounded that he would have chosen to join SIGRID OLSEN, since we were still small players in the larger scheme of the fashion hierarchy. When David and Peter asked me to interview him (though I suspect they had already made their decision), he was characteristically nonchalant.

I questioned him directly, but politely.

"So, Ed, what is it about our little company that attracts a person such as yourself? You were president of Perry Ellis and before that at Calvin Klein and Esprit. Why do you want to come to work at SIGRID OLSEN?"

Typically soft-spoken and always composed he said, "Well. It's a challenge. I don't really have to do this, but I want to. Y'all have done a great job so far, but you need some help to get to the next level."

I wasn't sure what the next level was, but I had the feeling that he did. I wanted to learn what he knew and was excited to be moving up in the apparel world. Soon after this, when I was in Dallas for business, Ed and his wife, Jon, offered to take me out to dinner. When they pulled up to my hotel in their Mercedes, I slipped in quietly, feeling small in the big state of Texas. To my relief, Jon was no Dallas debutante—she could not have been sweeter or more genuine, putting me right at ease. I smiled when she referred to her husband as "Eddie."

This marked the beginning of our intertwined lives. A lot happened in the next five years.

SIGRID OLSEN (the company and the person) underwent an extreme makeover while EMJIII was at the helm. Things moved so fast my head was spinning. We still kept our main offices in Massachusetts where they had been all along, but New York became the center of activity since that's where the action was.

Our newly renovated showroom on Seventh Avenue was featured on the cover of Interior Design magazine, and we hired a public relations team to represent the brand. I spent more and more time there, flying back and forth, racking up the Delta miles, and losing track of where I was. Eventually, we installed an office for me in the new showroom, much smaller than Ed's corner office, with the fancy built-in cabinets, groovy sound system, enormous desk, and executive washroom, but it made me feel like I had really arrived to be ensconced in the garment district. Now when I visited the city, it was no longer the New York of my childhood, but my *home*, someplace I really belonged.

In 1995, my star was very much on the rise. Ed had hired a publicist, and I began to mingle with the movers and shakers of the apparel world. I can't say I was ever part of the fashion elite. Those of us that had a thriving business at the midlevel, catering to real women at reasonable prices, never entered the rarified realm of hundred thousand-dollar fashion shows, multiple page spreads in Vogue and revealing pictures on Page Six of the New York Post. We had a small advertising budget compared to more prominent brands like Donna Karan, Ralph Lauren and Prada, but each season we squeaked out enough pages to be courted by magazines, and we enjoyed many of the associated perks.

At that point, I was in charge of media buying and creative direction for our ad campaigns, so I got invited to all the cocktail parties, resort weekends and other special events. It was time to get myself camera ready if I was going to be out there in public.

I had come a long way since my barefoot hippie days, but my preference was to keep my look unfussy and natural. I was forty before I ever had a pedicure or a salon cut, but in a few short years, I was on a first name basis with Robert, my hair stylist at Frederic Fekkai, and on a weekly manicure schedule. I learned how a little pampering makes a person feel important and breeds confidence. Slowly, I was succumbing to the rites of the affluent modern female.

I was feeling pretty good one evening when I was scheduled to go to a *Glamour Magazine* event, promoting their 60th anniversary. I knew only a few people and was shuttled around by my publicist, trying my best to look like I belonged there, even though I felt out of place among the glitterati. At one point, I was urged to take the stage for a photo op and found myself standing between Cheryl Teigs and Heidi Klum, feeling like a backwoods dwarf in a little black dress. I smiled for the camera and held my breath until I could step down off the platform and get the hell out of there.

Another time I was invited to join a large contingent from *Glamour* (again) for a two-day getaway at a luxurious Adirondack resort, all expenses paid. I was blown away to be included, but I had promised Brita, who was fifteen at the time and in boarding school, that I would finally be *home* for the weekend, and we could spend some time together. I had to decline. But then I remembered the invitation had been for two, so I asked if I could bring my daughter. "We'd love to have her come," said my ad rep, "I hope she likes the country."

She was thrilled. I always grasped any opportunity where I could mix family and work time since I had so little of the former and too much of the latter. I appreciated that Brita was always game to try anything and join me on odd outings where I might not have 100 percent of my attention focused on her. She never pouted or acted out. She just learned to listen, observe and enjoy the fruits of free travel. She accompanied me on dozens of photo shoots over the years, always befriending the stylist to get as close as possible to the jewelry, shoes and other accessories which were laid out on display for the model to wear. It was a little girl's dream. It made me feel better to know she was safe and close to me when I was away from home, even if that was only possible on certain trips like this. (Now that she is a New York stylist and event designer in her own right, I see how early exposure had unexpected benefits.)

When we arrived at the woodland retreat we were immediately swept up by the pristine beauty and the old-fashioned charm of the place, which had the feel of a very expensive campground. It was cool and overcast that weekend, and first thing we did was cross the lake in a small rowboat and hike through the woods on the other side. This was just what my spirit needed, and I was happy to see Brita enjoying herself with such a wholesome activity. As we relaxed in the refuge of nature, the stress of my life melted away.

This was not just any free trip. The publisher, associate publisher, and fashion editor were there with a handful of other advertisers like myself. They needed to get away from their hectic lives just as much as I did. All three of these women have moved on from this magazine to other positions elsewhere, but they are very well known, and I felt privileged to mix with them in such an intimate setting. They totally relaxed and let their guard down, because no one was watching way out here in the wilderness. We only had to devote about a half hour listening to their trend report and advertising pitch and the rest of the time was spent hiking, sleeping, or eating the amazing food that was served. I felt we were observing the female executive in her alternate habitat, at rest and at play.

That night, after dinner, we wound ourselves along a moonlit path to a campfire they had set up for us by the lake. There was chilled champagne and smores at the ready and after a generous dose of both, we began singing Broadway show tunes. I will never forget the ridiculously entertaining number that closed the evening. We were watching Glamour royalty…the publishing triumvirate—publisher, associate publisher and fashion director…standing up on a boulder belting out *"Mack the Knife"* after one-too-many glasses of champagne.

In those days, magazines were spending money freely. Things have changed dramatically, and it isn't as fun as it used to be. But I knew, even then, the extravagance was ridiculous. If you consider how few pages we bought in a year, the money spent entertaining us could have hardly been worth it. For me, just being seen in these major publications was a thrill.

I wanted to be proud of the images we presented. Now that we had national visibility, it was important for us to get the look of our ads to be more clean and sophisticated. Ed was a catalyst for this change, urging us to morph from a provincial, New England, girl-next-door look to that of an "aspirational brand", and he knew the people to do it. This meant finding a new art director, photographer and models, all located in New York. Ed was slowly changing the complexion of our organization, bringing us up-to-date and in-line with the rest of the industry.

It was heartening to have someone with his experience sit in on our design process and appreciate our work. He encouraged our team to elevate the quality and sophistication of the fashion in step with the rest of the industry. This didn't mean that we would be like everyone else, but, in order for the uniqueness of our clothes to stand out, we had to up our game. The decade of 1990-1999 brought a level of polish to the brand that catapulted us to the next level, just as Ed had predicted.

Doors were opening up for me every day, and I never hesitated to walk through, each one leading to a new world I had never imagined. The first door had opened to a factory screening my prints in Hong Kong, and now I was getting to work with amazing professionals in fashion, advertising and graphic design. I loved my role as Creative Director. It allowed me to manifest my vision, both in the design of the clothes and in the advertising images that presented them to the world.

In an effort to elevate the look of our brand, Ed pushed for a new approach for shooting our catalogs and advertising visuals. Since he had been doing this for ages, with companies much more prominent than mine, I respected his opinion. One of the first observations he made when he joined us surprised me though.

"You know what I find odd about this company, Sigrid?"

"Umm," I hesitated, certain it had something to do with my art or the way we approached our designs. "Well, I am not sure. What?"

"You have a hundred and fifty employees in two states and not one gay or person of color. Why is that?" An odd comment from a straight white guy from Dallas, but he had been in the business long enough to know that it was disproportionately populated by folks from the above categories. We had simply never had anyone fitting that description apply for a job. We wouldn't have hesitated to hire them. I was chagrined, especially considering my progressive upbringing, and we quickly got to work remedying this.

When Ed introduced me to Vincent, a new art director, who he recommended for the task at hand, he said, "He is a little unusual, but he's a true artist. I think you'll like him. "

The day I was scheduled to meet with Vincent, I was nervous, hoping that we would be able to relate to each other, as I always felt like a suburban housewife thrust into New York culture, even if he was there specifically to meet me. He walked in dressed completely in black, wearing his ever-present wool stocking cap over his shaved head and big black glasses, carrying a portfolio. He was definitely avant-garde, but immediately had me laughing with his quirky sense of humor. I liked him right away.

His studio was located on Little West Twelfth Street in the Meat-packing District, in the days when they were still packing meat there. (Now it has become more like an upscale shopping mall.) The first few times I visited his studio, I was repulsed by the pungent smell in the summer heat. It felt mildly dangerous walking those streets, especially if we had an early morning meeting and I had to wend my way through groups of ragged people who were making their way home from clubs or from the nearby all-night restaurant, *Florent*. I would ring Vincent when I arrived and, before long, we would be immersed in our current project, forgetting the bloody butcher stalls that surrounded us.

Vincent introduced me to a brilliant photographer, Michael, who had a dramatic flair and also dressed entirely in black with a stocking cap over a shaved head. I began to wonder if there was a wardrobe stylist somewhere who catered to gay creatives in lower Manhattan. We began to compile a small collaborative group and made huge strides polishing the look of our visuals together. I was turned on and loved this part of my job, away from the spreadsheets and calendar deadlines that governed the rest of my work life.

One of the first campaigns that Michael, Vincent and I shot together was with Patti Hansen, former supermodel and wife of the Rolling Stone's Keith Richards. We had rented a townhouse on lower Fifth Avenue for our location. Patti brought in her own hair stylist, and they spent the first two hours of the day reminiscing about old times, while I listened in wonder. Her girls were young then, and I marveled as she shared stories about ballet lessons and school projects, like an ordinary suburban mom. But that was exactly the reason we cast her in the role for this shoot. We wanted someone beautiful and glamorous, but with a natural, unaffected allure that women could relate to. Patti, with her easy smile and freckled complexion, was perfect.

Another time, we chose Hunter Reno, niece of ex-attorney general Janet Reno. A six-foot-tall Amazonian beauty with a gorgeous smile, she was also naturally appealing, athletic and strong. Her personality was just as un-self-conscious as her appearance, and I was enchanted right away. We had chosen her from headshots, but when she showed up, Vincent felt she needed something to freshen her look. When I arrived the morning of the shoot, he was all excited, eager to show me how Hunter had been transformed.

"We wanted her to look just like Jean Seberg from the 60s film *Breathless*. Doesn't she look fabulous?" Michael was also ardently expressing his approval. "You will die. She looks amazing."

I went to see what all the fuss was about. She was seated in the makeup chair touching her hair and gazing tentatively at her reflection in the mirror. Her hair was cut short, so short it was alarming, but as I studied her, I saw the genius in it. I loved it, and fortunately, so did she. The soft blonde spikes were like a halo around her flawless face. She felt like it completely revitalized her, and it did.

One of the first outfits we featured (probably the one that inspired the metamorphosis to French movie star) was a black and white striped jersey top very similar to the one Jean Seberg wore in the film. We shot her on the beach against an enormous red canvas that Vincent had ordered painted, just for the campaign. It was bold, and she looked like a free spirit, just like in *Breathless*. Vincent was beside himself, elated by the vision he had conjured.

We shot our Spring Collection that June in the Hamptons. Ed decided he wanted to supervise what was going on that day on the beach. After all, the budget was probably close to a hundred thousand for the whole production, and he was President. It was important that he be sure we were making the most of our money. The irony of this impulse was that he chose to fly from Manhattan by seaplane for the brief hour he spent with us on location. I'm not sure what this cost, but it seemed extravagant.

Ed was upbeat, captivated by memories of grander times. "This is nothing. I remember when we used to fly back and forth from Perry's (Ellis) estate on his private seaplane that he kept right there on his dock. Those were the days."

When he asked if I wanted to ride back to the city with him, I was intrigued. It had been a long day and I didn't relish the three-hour drive back to Manhattan. It was thrilling as we rose above the Atlantic, with Long Island a ribbon of land fading into the distance. The romance ended abruptly when I felt a wave of nausea overtake me, and I rested my head in my hands looking desperately at the floor until we landed thirty minutes later, missing the incredible vista entirely. I wasn't destined for such a lofty lifestyle.

The truth is…I wrestled with my ego the whole time my career was taking off. I worked hard to hang onto my humility while everyone else pushed me onto a pedestal.

In New York circles, I had the reputation of being "down to earth" and "accessible," while back at home my peers felt me lifting off to loftier heights, drifting away from them, becoming SIGRID OLSEN. It was as though my identity was beginning to bisect into two entities—one retained the essence of me and the other belonged to the company. As the brand gained notoriety, my personal life shifted to accommodate the weight of increased responsibility. More and more time was spent in New York, and I felt myself drift away from the things I knew would keep me grounded—time in nature, yoga, meditation, fun with friends, and quality time with my family.

Work became the center of my life. Many women entrepreneurs know the agony of being preoccupied with the dual role of parenting and running a company. I was a single parent with two children, not without some major painful events, causing me to feel guilty and inadequate much of the time.

It was a tricky paradox. With all the blossoming career success, failure still nagged at my heart. I came to realize that there is no substitute for spending actual time with those you not only love, but who you also are responsible for. The regret lingers long after the damage is done, and there is little one can do to rewind the clock and make it right.

So we proceed, doing the best we can under the circumstances. No one has the ideal set-up. The awareness I gleaned from my own childhood was also true for me as a mother and, as the cycle continues, it's passed to my children. *We learn as much from our parent's failings as we do from their successes.*

My intimate life was a shifting landscape as well. By the mid-nineties I was disillusioned and frustrated, having to balance work and parenting. Trying to please everyone was exhausting. I decided to simply try and be happy with what I had. Both my kids were in boarding school, things hadn't been easy, but they were still my primary focus and that was enough for now. I worked hard and in my spare time, I rekindled friendships at home, enjoying daily walks with one of my oldest friends, who lured me into power-walking four miles with her every day, and that soothed me. I felt virtuous setting aside time for myself, reestablishing a healthy habit to counteract the stress of my job.

It was just about this time that I met my second husband, Curtis. Our versions of this meeting differ slightly—he claimed we were deliberately set up by one of my designers and that I was the aggressor—but the point is that these things always seem to happen when you're not really looking for them.

Curtis represented a Spanish textile mill from which we bought fabric. He was visiting New York from Northern California, where he had his home and office. Traveling all over the world with his job, he pioneered a new fabric called *tencel* which was doing very well. He made frequent trips to New York to meet with designers and fabric buyers. I rarely met with fabric reps, but my team was in Massachusetts that day, so I agreed to meet with him instead. I'd also heard he was single and a nice guy, so when he arrived, I was mildly interested.

Greeting him in the conference room where he presented his swatches, we drifted into a comfortable conversation. (He said I flirted. I don't think so.) We talked about fashion, our jobs, and the fact that we were both single parents trying to juggle career and children. He was raising four kids on his own, so he had me beat. I was impressed.

I had just extracted myself from a deeply disappointing, four-year relationship which had gone on three and a half years too long. It was too much to be a parent and try to negotiate a new relationship, especially one with a narcissist who had never had children. I felt damaged and torn apart from having to justify why I couldn't put him first, or even second, on my list of priorities. By then, I was relieved it was over and happy to be free.

With Curtis, it was easy to open up. I felt like he could understand since he was living a life so similar to mine. "God, it's exhausting isn't it? The dating, the working, the trying to be a good parent. I'm over it."

He agreed. Little did I know at the time what a hard partier he was. Dating was only the half of it.

So here is the part that I claim was just a joke, and he remembers as a vaguely seductive:

"I have an idea that would take the pressure off—*you and I* should go out. You live in California, and I live in Massachusetts. It's perfect! We would never see each other!"

"Good idea," he replied as he packed up his sample cases and walked out the door.

It was months before I heard from him again. I had happily returned to my hectic life of work and parenting, content for the time being, without giving him more than a passing thought. My designers knew of him, because they had met him at a Paris Fabric fair, and so did Ed, who was charmed because he knew that, although he was now based in California, Curtis was a fellow Texan.

One day, we had the whole gang in the Massachusetts conference room for a design meeting, including Ed. The phone rang, and my assistant asked if I wanted to speak with a Curtis Sanders. I have no idea why she put the call through, since normally she would take a message if I was in a meeting. I picked up the phone, curious and slightly embarrassed.

"Hi, this is Sigrid."

"Hi, Sigrid. This is Curtis Sanders, from Tejidos Royo. Remember me? We met a while back in your showroom."

I looked around to see if anyone was listening. They all were. Ed eyes were fixed on me and he had a big grin on his face. "Oh please," I thought. "Now what do I do?"

"Yes, of course. What can I do for you?"

"Well, I was calling to see if you were going to be in Las Vegas next week for the apparel show? I think you have a booth there."

"Yes, I'll be there. Why?"

"I was hoping you might have time to come out and have a drink with me sometime. I'll be there for a couple of days. Does that work for you?"

"Sure, that will be fine." I tried to sound professional, mostly for the benefit of the multiple ears on my end of the phone call. "You can stop by the booth. I'll be there most of the show."

Flustered, I hung up the phone and turned back to seven curious faces around the conference table.

"What? We're just having a drink. It's nothing. Now let's get back to work."

My face felt hot and I knew it had to be flushed. I resumed my place as the center of attention for the meeting, but it was not because of my brilliant design leadership. In a quick attempt to turn the focus away from the phone call and my impending meeting/date, I picked up where we left off, reviewing samples for the upcoming Spring release. I had tons to do before Vegas, and Curtis Sanders was the last thing I wanted to spend time thinking about. The call had messed with my flow. If given the choice, I probably would have asked to take a message.

It's a funny anecdote, because in later years, when Curtis and I were married, and he'd call me at the office, when I answered, invariably the conversation would begin like this:

I'd say, "I'm in a meeting."

He'd say: "Why did you answer then?"

I'd give a small laugh and reply: "Because I thought it would be either important or quick. Let's face it…I am *always* in a meeting. My day is just one long string of meetings. So which is it? Important or quick?" It became a joke between us.

Our booth at the Vegas show was busy, and we had a steady stream of customers to greet and charm. It's a tiring process, very repetitive, and after a few days of this dog and pony show, I was always grateful that sales were not my fulltime occupation. By the end of the week, we were all slightly delirious, more than ready for our "wrap party"—an intimate group dinner at a fancy restaurant, courtesy of EMJIII.

By five o'clock, I began to vaguely wonder what had become of Curtis Sanders. Days had passed, and the show was wrapping up in a few hours, but still there was no sign of him. Just as I was gathering my belongings and preparing to leave, he sauntered into our booth and asked if I might have time for that drink now. Inwardly, I rolled my eyes, not feeling all that psyched to be available after all this time, but as I hesitated, trying to decide what to do, everyone in my booth was gaping at me expectantly, "Go ahead, we can handle this." Ed was practically pushing me out the door. "Okay. Okay. I'm going!" To Curtis, I murmured, "Let me get my things." I said my goodbyes around the room and promised to meet them all later for dinner at the Luxor Hotel.

Curtis and I found a seat at the hotel bar and settled in for an hour or so of conversation before I had to scoot off to my hotel room and change for dinner. I ordered a white wine but had to confess that I was suffering from some kind of strange affliction that caused me to sneeze whenever I drank alcohol of any kind, so I wasn't much of a drinker. He, on the other hand, had enjoyed a lifelong love affair with the stuff and confessed to me later, once he had quit altogether, that my admission was very close to being a deal-breaker that evening in Las Vegas.

We found that we had a lot to talk about. The hour went by quickly and soon it was time to go. I think we were both surprised at the common ground we discovered as we tiptoed around the perimeter of our personal landscapes. It seemed too early to part ways, so I proffered an unexpected dinner invitation, sure that if I walked into the Luxor with *this* uninvited guest, everyone was sure to approve. As it turned out, he was scheduled to fly out that evening, so he had to decline.

This was probably a good thing. With three thousand miles between us, our early relationship developed slowly, mostly on the phone. There was no email or texting yet, so we would spend hours just talking. It was several weeks before we saw one another again. After dozens of phone calls, we finally scheduled a time to have our first real date. I flew to California and we spent our first weekend together in a Sausalito hotel, overlooking San Francisco Bay. The second date was in Paris, where we both traveled twice a year for *Premier Visione*, the global fabric fair. *Tejidos Royo* had a booth there, and Curtis was their US representative. If it sounds fun and romantic, it was.

The viability of this bicoastal relationship was made possible by the fact that we both traveled so much and often to the same places: New York, Paris, Dallas, Las Vegas, L.A. For both of us, managing single parenting, a demanding career and a relentless travel schedule, left little time for romance. But somehow, we prevailed. Once his kids were grown and out of the house, Curtis gave up his fabulous home in Marin County, moved to New York to open the first U.S. office for his Spanish employer, and we cohabited for the first time.

Both of us had businesses centered in New York, so it was natural to settle there together. We found a funky little apartment literally two blocks away from my grandmother's Murray Hill flat where I had spent much of my childhood. On the fourth floor of an old brownstone, it was one of two apartments above a set of offices. Nothing ever was quite right with the place, but we loved it. Charming, but odd, it had an elevator that opened directly into our apartment that could only be accessed after walking up one flight of stairs. If that were not absurd enough, it was further complicated by the fact that if anyone ever happened to forget to close the expandable gate, then it was stopped in its tracks, causing us to have to walk down three flights just to correct the situation.

After a year or two, we moved to a brand new, high-rise building with breathtaking views of the Empire State Building—a real-life New York adventure. We stayed there for about three years until 911 happened, and we wanted no part of living on the 45th floor of a luxury apartment building in Manhattan.

Everything was moving so fast, only occasionally did I stop and breathe, and allow myself a moment to absorb all that was happening.

September 11th was an all-encompassing, heartbreaking, tragically beautiful, game changer. It highlighted our communal need for one another, our human tendency towards kindness and a genuine love for our United States of America.

No matter how skeptical, alternative, liberal or anti-establishment any of us had ever been, our national solidarity was galvanized by this event. Emotionally, it took its toll. I could not ignore the gravity and preciousness of life itself and I was overwhelmed by an intense affection for my family and my coworkers. Nothing would ever be the same.

Meanwhile, life went on. For a while, it was difficult to find meaning in the fashion world. It paled in comparison to the momentous universal loss we all shared. Looking back, it's hard to believe we recovered. I had to find a way to integrate the deeper human experience into my already overstuffed psyche. But after a while, life fell back into a familiar rhythm, the pain faded, and we lost ourselves once again in the demands of day-to-day business.

MY LIFE IN MONTAGE
personal photo collection

Father and daughter 1959

*Silver Pin made for Lucia,
by Alexander Calder*

*With parents and grandparents
NYC, Christmas 1953*

*With mother and grandmother in
Copenhagen c. 1954*

*Lucia coming to America
in 1952 via ship (in a bikini)*

Early childhood in Connecticut 1957

*Resting on one of our many Danish
Modern chairs c. 1965*

*My father as a young Navy man
and artist in Pearl Harbor
just before bombs fell*

*New siblings:
Lisa and Danny c. 1968*

Early Influences

A likeness, sculpted by my mother

My mother's taste in decorating was unusually creative.

Oak door, hand-carved for my parents by husband, Steve from my design. c. 1978.

Above: Parents beatnik party c. 1961.

With step-sister Martha- two girls happily thrown together (with kittens).

My mother, Lucia in her happy place—on the beach.

On horseback during my teen years as a stable hand. Loved this guy, Rex.

Acapulco Gold poster, purchased for me by my mother c. 1969.

Early cookbook created as a result of our lunch program in art school

Hippie Days with my first husband, Steve, my grandparents and mother

At home at "Dogpatch" —little house in the woods in Rockport MA.

Grandmother, Rose with newborn baby, Erik

New mother with baby Erik c. 1979 (photo credit: Peter Ruchman)

Erik in his handmade coat c. 1982

Erik, age 2

Baby Brita in the basket I brought her in to craft fairs with me

Baby Brita, playing a wooden drum with her Dad.

Artisan Entrepreneur

Stamping with hand carved stamps

*Infant Brita in her
hand printed baby bunting*

*Early potato print pattern with
egrets and marsh grass motifs*

*Print process from mock-up to final
product*

*Early prints from
Segrets Sun Prints Collection*

*Our very first Segrets Sun Prints
retail store—Rockport, MA 1986*

Hand carved stamps showing the positive /negative imagery

*Early trade show booth for
Segrets Sun Prints c. 1987*

Segret's Sun Prints

Silkscreening in progress in Hong Kong c. 1986

Silkscreened Bird Print

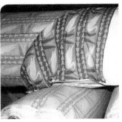
Finished rolls of silkscreened fabric

Mother, Lucia loved all my designs, this one from my line of "Sea Tees"

Brita wearing Segrets Kids with roll of fabric c. 1987

My original partners: Peter (left) and David (right)

Example of Spring 1989 print swatch roll invented by Peter

Peter Wagner wearing Segrets rugby shirt with white bird print

SIGRID OLSEN
The Brand

My original design team c.1994 (l. to r.) Elaine, Dorian, me, Nancy, Sylvia, Lenard with photo of Patti Hansen in the background

With art director, Vincent Gagliostro c. 1994

Hosting a fashion show at the Aventura Mall in Miami

Posing with models wearing my original art silk blouses. (I am standing on a milk crate!)

My appearance on "Martha" November 2007

Toronto Film Festival 2008 with director, Marc Levin at the premiere of documentary "Schmatta"

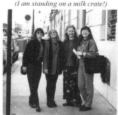

My design team in Paris

Fashion show a Nordstrom

Fashion show at Bloomingdales, featuring tencel™ fabric

Ad Campaigns

Model Hunter Reno
after Jean Seberg haircut

ad in Glamour Magazine
East Hampton, L.I.
Photo Credit: Michael O'Brien

One of my faves...
Mykonos, Greece
ad by Laspata Decaro

Fall photo shoot
Aspen, Colorado
ad by Laspata DeCaro

Location photo shoot
Capri, Italy
photo credit: Hugh Stewart

Linen Embroidered Coat
Crane Beach, MA
ad by Laspata Decaro

Bus kiosk ad NYC
Laspata DeCaro

Heidi Klum
Elle cover in our blue blouse
(but who would notice it?)

Location photo shoot
Harbour Island, Bahamas
photo credit: Hugh Stewart

Embracing Color

A sampling of the hand-carved rubber stamps in my collection

Original Painting "Pale Lotus" with inscription

In my Rocky Neck Gallery with my paintings and hand-painted pottery Photo Credit: Paul Lyden

Hand-painted pottery, work-in-progress Photo Credit: Jody Hilton for NY Times 2008

A look inside my Sarasota Gallery Pillows and pottery 2014

Samples of colorful hand-painted mini bowls

Hand-painted pottery and greeting cards in gallery

Curtis hanging artwork in Rocky Neck Gallery 2012

Demonstrating how to carve rubber stamps during an art workshop

Galleries & Retail Stores

*The SIGRID OLSEN art
Rocky Neck Gallery*

*Watercolor print drum light from
SIGRID OLSEN retail store*

*One of the 54 SIGRID OLSEN
retail store locations the U.S.*

*Inside the Hingham, Massachusetts
SIGRID OLSEN store (now closed)*

*Customer seating area in SIGRID
OLSEN retail store with personal
vacation photos and artwork on wall*

*Posing with one of my paintings in
my house before it sold*

*SIGRID OLSEN bath towel with
coordinating artwork*

*SIGRID OLSEN HOME
showroom NYC*

*SIGRID OLSEN HOME
sampling of towels in our
NYC showroom*

Tulum Retreat

The aquamarine water of Tulum.   Casa Magna Tulum   The Mayan ruins of Tulum

Palapa- Si'an Kan Reserve   On the first retreat 2009   The beauty of nature

Breathtaking sunrise   Foot bath outside yoga studio   Sunrise Salutation

Life Redesigned

On Siesta Key Beach
Sarasota FL
photo credit: Troy Plota

My home practice
on self-designed yoga mat
by Whimsy Rose

My favorite cotton beach tunic
SIGRID OLSEN STUDIO
photo credit: Bryan Kasm

At home in my
SIGRID OLSEN SIGNATURE
embroidered cotton kurta
photo credit: Bryan Kasm

From my Dinner Party photo shoot
SIGRID OLSEN SIGNATURE
photo credit:
This Good Life Photography

Dinner Party photo shoot
SIGRID OLSEN SIGNATURE
photo credit:
This Good Life Photography

With daughter, Brita in NYC
SIGRID OLSEN SIGNATURE
photo credit: Tory Williams

Juicing for retreat goers
Sarasota FL
photo credit: Troy Plota

Yacht Club Luncheon photo shoot
SIGRID OLSEN SIGNATURE
photo credit:Jenny Acheson

The Big Push

"Remember. Amateurs built the ark.
Professionals built the Titanic."
—Anonymous

My job was so absorbing, I began to forget who I was outside of work. My identity became hopelessly intertwined with the business. It was like quicksand, once I stepped in, it was hard to extricate myself. The brand was swallowing me up. I found myself joining the chorus of voices, whose main goal was to enhance the company's brand recognition, referring to myself in the third person:

"That's so Sigrid."

"These colors really have a Sigrid Olsen feel."

"How can we capture the Sigrid Olsen spirit with our ad campaign?"

We were so focused on our work, almost incestuous in the closed circle we had become, that we weren't aware that our reputation extended far beyond our small fashion world. Soon after Ed came on board, we caught the attention of apparel giant Liz Claiborne (the corporation, not the person), which occupied several floors in the same building where our New York offices were located.

Ed was a great networker, making the first overture with the corporation's top executives. This was followed by several weeks of scrutiny, with teams of "suits" walking through our showroom, studying the latest collection hanging on our racks. They were very complimentary, praising the colors, the quality, and the accessible price point.

"How are you able to do all this for the price? The collections look like "bridge" (a high-end apparel classification), but they are so affordable!"

Their incredulity surprised me. "It's what we have always done. We work together and choose the best fabrics, embellishments and pay attention to every little detail."

It seemed like the most natural thing in the world to me. Since this was my only job ever in the apparel industry, I had nothing to compare it to. The process was natural, but not effortless. It was accomplished by a massive group effort. The incredibly dedicated staff had grown up with the company, many had been there since its infancy.

Good design doesn't necessarily cost more. It just takes creativity, commitment and a shit ton of hard work. This was inherent in my work ethic and that of those around me. My design team constantly amazed and inspired me, never settling for just okay, always striving for the best. There were many times when I would approve a print, a fabrication, or sketch only to be told by the designer, "No. I think I need to work on it some more", to the annoyance of those managing the ever-tyrannical design calendar. We prided ourselves on doing the best we possibly could. Creativity was the easy part.

The stressful part of fashion design is not coming up with original ideas. What drives designers crazy is the constraint of tight deadlines that are virtually impossible to meet. This fact is universal and seemingly constant for every fashion person I know. We are always rushing to get work done, with no hope of finishing on time. It was discouraging and eroded any sense of joy we might have found in the task at hand.

At SIGRID OLSEN in those days, coming up with new concepts was our collective duty. Fortunately, we had the tools, if not the luxury of time. We had imagination. We traveled. We constantly strove to be better. The company wisely devoted an enormous chunk of our operating budget to travel—Paris, London, L.A., Italy, Palm Beach—all to ensure that we were not only aware of all the latest trends, but that we would have a rich supply of fresh concepts and an expansive view of the world.

While we continued to be immersed in the day-to-day design cadence, the looming prospect of the Liz acquisition was becoming increasingly real. Ed was having more closed-door meetings, with David, Peter and various executives from the LCI corporation. They wined and dined us, and I admit I was flattered by their attention. I was invited to a private dinner with the CEO, where he questioned me about my life goals and design philosophy. Being the people pleaser I am, I strove to say and do the right thing, be smart and witty and, of course, show that I would be easy to work with. They needed my cooperation, but the truth is, I owned less than ten percent of the company, so mine was not the deciding vote.

And here it is—the pivotal moment in my story—which would shape my career for decades to come, but I was too naive to realize it.

At the time my desire to succeed and be recognized as a major designer was in sharp contrast to my natural tendency to keep my ego in check. I found it impossible to resist the delight of being wanted. I felt my star rising, and in many ways, the upward move felt inevitable. Like so many other times in my career, the momentum felt unstoppable.

The energy of the companies' merger was gaining speed, and it felt like the best choice was just to let it happen. Again, life was presenting a lesson but, being immersed in the moment, I had no outside perspective with which to judge the outcome.

Eventually I was presented with their proposal. One key factor (the real issue that gave me pause) stood out sharply. My name was the trademark that LCI was obtaining along with the infrastructure and business we had built. Not Peter's. Not Ed's or David's. Mine. "In perpetuity" is how the contract read. As I read the words, I felt my heart thump in my chest. It was the eleventh hour. The sale was positioned to go through in just a few days and, try as I did, I could not imagine a scenario where I would speak up and say that it was unacceptable. So, even though I wrestled with the notion of giving up my name, I signed.

When people question me about this turn of events, asking why I owned so little of my company's stock when my name was on the label, my answer is this: "Keep in mind, I rode my bike to my very first business meeting. I had no experience, no prior job in the industry, invested zero dollars, and frankly, was just happy to have a job, doing what I loved to do." I was well compensated for my job over the years, but my shares in the company were minimal. It was a very different set of circumstances, fifteen years later, when I finally had the opportunity to regain my name again. But in 1999, I was an employee of the Liz Claiborne Corporation (LCI).

I naively believed that nothing would change, that LCI would simply give us the financial and operational strength to take the business to the next level. But, little by little, everything changed. Within a few short weeks, Ed resigned. David and Peter took their shares and started new ventures. I was left as the only original founder of the company and became Creative Director, reporting to an unfamiliar Liz Claiborne executive who would serve as our president until a permanent one could be found.

The next period was not unlike the first weeks of a new marriage or leaving home to go off to college. There were new people to meet, meetings to attend, systems to learn. The biggest challenge was teaching the folks at Liz Claiborne the ways of SIGRID OLSEN. We had developed our own way of doing things; even our organizational structure was different. And it was working—in many ways, more effectively than anyone at LCI had seen. That's why, years later, when the harsh winds of corporate intervention came in and completely revamped our familial culture, we were all literally blown away.

Learning the corporate ropes took a little getting used to. It was overwhelming, but I enjoyed the challenge. This was a truly rigorous training ground. I looked at it as another step in my education, like an on-the-job MBA. For some reason, it's in my nature to take pleasure in being tested, to measure my competence against a greater field. Up until this point, I was content with my entrepreneurial mission and my design duties, but now there was an immense world of options at my fingertips. It got my engine humming to think of the creative possibilities.

But things were never as simple as I thought they'd be. In the wake of Ed's departure, after the merger, there was a real leadership void, which precipitated a desperate scramble to assemble a team that could assist in the assimilation of SIGRID OLSEN into the larger, complex entity. I began to see very quickly that I would have little input in the selection of our management team. Instead, new people were thrust at me in every area. I gathered immediately that growth and profit would be our main objectives, not yet grasping what we would sacrifice to get there.

My first entree into the inner realms of corporate financial planning was the quarterly "Strat Plan" meeting that had everyone around me "knitting an anxiety sweater" (a phrase my friend Sabine uses that cracks me up). It was an event the likes of which I had never experienced before. When presented with the spectacle looming in the not-so-distant future, I had to confess, I had no idea what a "Strat Plan" was.

Puzzled, I asked my new boss what was required and why was everyone so wound up about it?

She looked at me as though, at just that moment, she realized what a long road she had ahead of her to teach me the ways of corporate hierarchy. "*Strat plan* is short for strategic plan. They happen every quarter. It's the way in which top management gets a snapshot of every division in the company. We work to present our individual P&L's, and the top executives give us their feedback."

The preparation was rigorous, with very specific goals and projections applied to things we really could not predict. I had made hundreds of design and sales presentations before, but this was an entirely different animal. For weeks, the finance people were harried, spreadsheets were everywhere, and I channeled my alter ego, the academic overachiever.

"This should be pretty simple," I told myself. Again, I was wrong.

It was never simple. During the nine years we were under the stewardship of LCI, I sat through dozens of these meetings and, though I always tried to lend creative authenticity to the presentation, the spreadsheet mentality prevailed. I quickly learned how to interpret a P&L (profit and loss statement), which was a point of pride for our CEO. More than once, he introduced me as "Sigrid Olsen, designer, artist and Creative Director who knows her way around a P&L".

In the first months of our merger, we received lots of praise from all around. Not only had we developed a great brand out of keen instincts and sheer will, but we were known to be smart, kind and easy to work with. It was a boost to our collective ego to be recognized for everything we had accomplished. Now, we were compelled to turn that excellence into profit. This would turn out to be a rigorous effort and the education of a lifetime.

It was a heady time at Liz Claiborne, Inc. as the CEO pushed for top line growth and achieved it by acquiring dozens of companies over the next several years. SIGRID OLSEN was only the first in a series of at least twenty big deals, and we watched as our place in the larger enterprise became less and less prominent.

Soon after our assimilation into the LCI stable, two more companies followed close behind. I felt the warmth of the designer spotlight shift away from me and onto the newer acquisitions, like an only child suddenly getting a very cute baby sister (or two). The first was Lucky Brand, a contemporary denim line from L.A., which upped the hipness factor at LCI somewhat, and then the next one, Juicy Couture, sent it into the stratosphere.

Each of those brands was founded by a pair of design entrepreneurs that brought the same kind of passion to their ventures as I did. While the thrill of being part of such a powerhouse was intoxicating, none of us were prepared for the frustrations of corporate life. The endless meetings, financial jargon, the pecking order, the demand for growth and loss of individual culture—all of this was exasperating. We had built our businesses through sheer grit and instinct and now had to conform to practices that did not resonate.

After the first three, dozens more acquisitions followed. At its height LCI was the parent to over forty-five different labels, including the expansive namesake brand, Liz Claiborne, and its offshoot divisions. Dana Buchman (founded years before under the LCI umbrella), Ellen Tracy, C&C California, Prana (yoga-wear), Mexx (A Dutch mega-brand) and Kate Spade were among the many companies that were part of this huge conglomerate. Although it was exciting to belong to something so enormous and significant, the number of moving parts to manage, plus the friction of conflicting agendas between divisions, eventually destroyed the enterprise from the inside.

It was a wild ride, dangerously out of control at times, but also exhilarating. SIGRID OLSEN was seeing phenomenal sales growth and expansion into other product lines, like handbags, jewelry, eyewear and bedding. We were well established in most major department stores—Macy's, Parisian, Belk's, Dillard's, Nordstrom, Dayton Hudson, Marshall Fields, Saks, Bloomingdale's—even though our small specialty business had waned. Then, in the span of three years, from 2003-2006, we opened 54 SIGRID OLSEN company-owned retail stores across America.

Having my own brick and mortar space to feature my designs was a dream come true. The first one opened in the Chestnut Hill Mall, outside of Boston, right in my back yard. I'd worked with the company's architectural design team to inspire the aesthetic, so I looked forward to the grand opening with anxious anticipation. Everything was perfect: the chunky wooden shelves, white walls, neat rows of merchandise, oversized baskets and wooden troughs for display, spacious fitting rooms, efficient cash wrap, and of course, my name over the door.

As I took it all in, though, I felt a hollow ache forming deep in my gut. So many people had worked so hard to get this accomplished, and yet, I had to fight back tears. Everyone looked at me expectantly, so I conjured a big smile and kept it there for the duration of the opening event. I should have been thrilled, but I felt empty. The space had no soul.

But this train had left the station. The design was in place, twelve more leases were signed, and the store construction machine was set into motion. So, I let myself be swept up into the momentum and threw myself into making them as successful as possible. I visited as many as I could manage, always encouraging the manager and staff to be upbeat while channeling their own intuitive desire to connect with the women who shopped there.

"It's not about clothes." I shared my personal philosophy with them during group sessions, in an attempt to give them something deeper to aspire to. "It is about well-being—making each customer feel welcome. They should come out of the fitting room feeling good about themselves—comfortable, feminine, happy. That's what drives me when I design, and I hope you can carry that message here."

We had some amazing store managers that really got it. Not only could they sell, but they motivated their staff to treat their job as something more like a mission. Those were the successful ones. They brought something to the retail venture that transcended commerce. They were human and empathetic and carried the deeper message to their work, like a personal calling.

The human bond that I made with my own staff, the store personnel and, ultimately, with my customers was the true measure of what I gained from my tenure at Liz. It was a real growth experience, not just on the spreadsheet, but in my heart as well.

I loved and respected the people in our retail division, but I was still troubled by the store design itself. It didn't embody the feel of the brand. None of the quirky creativity that, in my opinion, was central to my identity was evident in the upscale cookie-cutter walls that bore my name. I mentioned this to the Liz retail team and they understood. It did feel soulless, but no one had a solution. Once things were in motion at LCI, it was nearly impossible to change course.

Then one day I read an article about the architectural firm behind the *Anthropologie* stores. The founder of the firm, Ron Pompei, brought his sensibility as an artist and sculptor to his retail store design. I was intrigued by the philosophy behind the design, which he called "C3: culture, commerce and community." Here was someone who saw beyond the brick-and-mortar, with insight into the customer as a human being.

I started feeling a familiar restlessness brewing inside me, like an itchiness in my arms. I decided to "go rogue" on this one. Normally, I would have gone through the proper channels to bring my idea to the VP of retail and to the president over my brand. But my instincts told me to connect, person-to-person with Ron Pompei. So, I quelled my fears of retribution from the bigwigs at Liz, and I called him.

"Hi. My name is Sigrid Olsen. You may have heard of me, or maybe not."

Silence. I guess not.

"I am a fashion designer and my company is part of the Liz Claiborne Corporation."

"Oh, yes. OK. What can we do for you?"

I launched into my story, explaining how we were in the process of building a number of retail stores across the country, but I felt something was missing. I felt ballsy and timid at the same time, unsure that someone of his intellect and stature would want to work with me, and especially a company that was clearly unsophisticated in comparison. I know now that business is business, and we had a potential project to bring to the table, so he was all ears. He gave me his best inspirational pitch, and it turned out we were more like-minded than I thought. I felt at home again. I was talking to an artist. I hadn't realized how much I missed that. Imagination, creativity, innovation were topics of interest to both of us, not just profit margins, org charts and productivity.

Once a deal was struck, it was a struggle matching the two corporate cultures, but somehow, miraculously, we did it. After much negotiation, we launched into the second phase of the SIGRID OLSEN store design. The concept was brand new. I have to credit the open-mindedness of the LCI retail division for allowing this pivot so late in the game. It felt like an incredible vote of confidence in me and my brand.

The store design was ambitious, conceptually. The floor plan was devised around the idea that it should feel like entering my home. The facade was like a front porch and just inside was a comfy sitting area with books and magazines. My vacation photos and paintings were framed on the wall above the banquette and sheer linen curtains were draped across the opening to the display window. This unorthodox use of space went against everything a seasoned retailer would prescribe—the real estate closest to the store entrance is sacrosanct and should house merchandise for sale. To assign it to a seating area was a self-indulgent waste. But they let me do it. I was so happy to see how it gave everyone an instant cue to relax and stay for a while. Keeping customers in the store longer was one of the key objectives that this new approach was meant to accomplish.

Another intention was to reveal that I was an artist as well as a fashion brand. My watercolor washes were used on the translucent drum lights above the front desk, as well as the subtly toned ceramic tile on the surface of the cash wrap. The rear of the store was meant to evoke an artist's studio, with stacks of tee shirts and sweaters displayed in the drawers of an architectural flat file with large industrial pendants casting light from above. Everything had the luster of age, even though it was brand new, giving the customers a sense that they had left the mall and entered a new environment—one designed to both stimulate the senses and soothe the ruffled soul.

Who knew that in three years' time, the stores would be emptied, everything sold, right down to the hangers, beautiful pendant lamps and the art on the wall as well. Even I was unaware that the integrity of my dream was slipping through my fingers as I rose to the top of my field.

The liaison with Pompei Designs felt like a huge win at the time. I had succeeded in raising the creativity quotient in a very real way, and I was delighted. The crowning point of the store redesign was the construction of our New York flagship store in Soho. Every square foot of it (and there were a few thousand) was beautiful. The building itself spoke to the original turn of the century architecture of lower New York. Located on West Broadway, between Prince and Spring Streets, it was an expensive, (overly) ambitious location. Inside were artistic touches, beyond the homey decor specified in the blueprints, such as the two-story elevator enclosure that was wall-papered in my original print design and "found" pieces of furniture—antique armoires, tables, and shelves—that gave a luxe authenticity to the various rooms. The space attracted attention from the media, and on one occasion, we were visited by a group of international retail design students, who came to us for inspiration. It was all pretty exciting.

During this time, we had a succession of presidents assigned to oversee our division. I was constantly educating my bosses, trying to keep the integrity of the brand as the corporation intervened more and more. When we worked together, boosted by optimism and success, I felt as though anything was possible.

I had a vision and a team that could make it happen. At the tail end of Ed's reign, we had found a new advertising firm, Laspata/Decaro, whom I adored. I met the two founders, Charles and Rocco, during a cocktail party for Harper's BAZAAR on the Upper East Side. I was instantly smitten with Charles when we both sneaked out onto the balcony for a cigarette. In those days I was a social smoker. The best part about this furtive activity was how conversations hatched when small groups of us fringe-smokers broke off from the sometimes stifling boredom of cocktail party small talk.

I love these guys, even to this day. It was a privilege to work with them and a joy as well, because so much of our day was spent laughing. They are brilliant and funny and full of passion. We traveled to fabulous locations like Aspen, Palm Springs, Old San Juan and Montauk, but my favorite was Mykonos, a trip that almost didn't happen.

This was in the days when we spent six figures on an ad campaign, with media buys in Elle, Oprah, Vogue, Glamour, Martha Stewart, Harper's Bazaar and Marie Claire. We always searched for unusual, beautiful locations and models who epitomized the easy elegance that my customers would find aspirational, so shooting Eugenia Silva in Mykonos fit the bill perfectly. As soon as the idea was presented, I was captivated. I envisioned stark white, stucco walls and bright blue sky over azure water—a perfect backdrop for my colorful Spring Collection. But to my boss, it seemed like an unnecessary extravagance. To try and conserve, we compared numbers with what she proposed as a cheaper option in Florida. But I was stubborn. I set to work, figuring out how to make the Mykonos trip happen. My counter proposal: I would take a personal vacation, paying for my own travel and hotel lodging to save money. Our model lived in Spain, so it would actually be cheaper to have her come to Greece than to America. These two factors caused the bottom line to come in just under the Florida option, so off we went.

It *was* extravagant, and possibly unnecessary, but it was the best ad campaign we ever did. I got the thrill of my life when the whole montage went up on an enormous billboard in Times Square. One of the perks of being part of LCI was being able to take part in things like this—they had leased a grouping of seven outdoor images, right on Broadway and 42nd street. My dad was so thrilled that he took a photo of himself in front of it, arms spread wide with a huge grin, and sent it to me before I ever had a chance to see it in person. It made me happy to see his delight.

Meanwhile the impact of the SIGRID OLSEN product line was expanding. We partnered with the Liz Accessory design team to develop a line of gorgeous leather handbags and jewelry. I entered into this collaboration skeptically; worried that the need to appeal to a mass audience would cheapen the brand and that the quality I expected from us would be sacrificed for affordable price points. We worked together for months, refining color and pattern, choosing materials and providing original ideas and personal loves for inspiration. Once the samples started to flow in, I had to admit I was impressed. The talent of that team did not disappoint. To me, it seemed like they worked some sort of alchemist's magic to transform an array of accessories, from costume jewelry to handbags and winter scarves, into stylish, elegant things I would be happy to wear. They captured my color sense and artistic viewpoint, so all the pieces punctuated the clothing beautifully, and added dimension to our in-store displays.

Next, we signed with a licensee for Home Furnishings: bedding, tabletop and bath linens. I was thrilled, because home décor is a personal love of mine, almost more captivating than fashion. Like everything corporate, though, there were rules to be learned, merchandising and production issues to be solved and, most challenging of all, proper retail outlets to engage. The opening of our Home showroom was a big deal for me. Not only did we debut an impressive collection of colorful beds, bath towels, shower curtains, placemats and decorative pillows, but it was staged in such a naturally elegant way, I could imagine myself happily living in the space. I adopted many of the duvets, towels and sheets into my own home and enjoyed them for many years, in fact I still do. Shortly after this, we added eyewear to our design offerings and were actively on the hunt for other avenues of distribution.

The brand kept growing, excitement was building, and I was carried along by this rushing current of my budding passion. It was all push, push, push with little time for reflection.

~ 160 ~

Cancer as Catalyst

*"Life is about not knowing—having to change,
taking the moment, and making the
best of it, without knowing what's going to happen next.
Delicious ambiguity."*
—Gilda Radner

As if life wasn't chaotic enough, in the fall of 2004, I was diagnosed with breast cancer. Little did I know that this leave of absence would foreshadow the permanent separation that occurred 3 years later when my company closed. It gave me a much-needed opportunity to slowly disentangle myself from the stranglehold my business had on me.

At the time I was on the go constantly. Unknowingly, I had set the outrageous pace that was now expected of me. I would never have slowed down if I hadn't been forced to. Having to tend to my body opened a window to a new way of life.

Even today, I see how often I am faced with significant situations in my life that underscore this same theme: My spirit needs one thing, but my personality insists on another. In the end, circumstances prevail, and I am compelled to have compassion for myself, taking time out for self-care. In other words: shit just happens, and I choose how to deal with it. If I don't listen to my soul when it whispers, it will start to scream. Karma always catches up.

It caught up with me when I was at the apex of my career, with two children and not much time for myself. My diagnosis came during a particularly hectic design season, where we were managing lots of change, and the workplace was particularly prickly. I was deeply embroiled in managing multiple agendas, still having trouble letting go of everything after our corporate merger.

Cancer was the last thing I needed. Or so I thought.

Being diagnosed doesn't happen all at once. In reality, it's a long drawn out process that takes months to unfold. Most who have traveled this road know exactly what I mean. First, it's the "questionable" mammogram. Then the follow-up mammogram, that leads to the ultra-sound, which is also inconclusive. Oh, and three afternoons away from work. Dressing, undressing, waiting, more waiting, literally getting poked and prodded by multiple hands, needles and machines. Suddenly, there is way too much attention being paid to a part of your body that used to be fun and even useful in the past.

I was (and still am) a very busy lady, so I had put off getting a mammogram for too many years before the fateful day I received the news that something was wrong. That was my first mistake. Fortunately, once all the tests were in, I still was at stage zero (DCIS-ductal carcinoma in situ) and no real harm was done. We caught it early. My life was never in imminent danger, but it was still agonizing.

Cancer is a deep-dive into the medical abyss, no matter how excellent the care. It is as though an omnipresent entity has taken over your life. After multiple x-rays, an ultra-sound, an MRI, two needle biopsies, and 2 lumpectomies, I still was faced with having to choose a mastectomy. No matter how casual I sound now, I can recall the first time I heard the "m" word. It went through me like a shot.

I took the call in my office on a rainy November afternoon, hoping that the results of my lumpectomy would be the end of this ordeal, but instead, it was just the beginning. I hung up the phone and rejoined my design meeting stunned and completely distracted. I felt like a woman in a stupor, a soulless body filled with dust.

But I was well practiced at putting things on the back burner and before long I just became absorbed in the moment and postponed thinking about it until I got home. Then I collapsed and unraveled in the safety of my own four walls.

I know that having great medical care is important. It took me a little while to find the right combination of doctors. I lived in Hamilton, Massachusetts at the time, which is about an hour from Boston (if traffic was merciful) where my initial diagnosis and follow up care took place. As I shuttled from clinic, to hospital, to doctor's office, I tried in vain to keep my equilibrium and a solid sense of self. I did not want to become a simple statistic, a number on a chart.

Slowly, I began to sense that was exactly what I had become. The decision-making was a really hard process, even for me, a designer who was accustomed to making snap decisions at the drop of a hat, based purely on gut instinct.

The next step was to research the options for breast reconstruction. My first ever contact with a plastic surgeon made me feel:

a. Stupid, for asking questions.
b. Inexperienced, for never having had a mastectomy before.
c. Vain, for caring what I would look like afterwards.
d. Defeated, after the appointment.
e. Determined to find a better option.

I decided to do more research and get a "second opinion". So, I enlisted the help of friends, many of whom had brushed with cancer either themselves or through a family member. I even saw a therapist to talk through my feelings, which helped clarify my focus. Eventually, I was steered towards a team of doctors right in my backyard. It turned out Salem Hospital, twenty minutes from my home, was excellent, and my doctors were amazing. It is ironic that Boston is considered the pinnacle of medical progress, but the care I received in this mid-sized, suburban hospital was perfect for me.

The surgery was long. After nine hours, my family became worried, but it's simply a painstaking process. The beauty of it was that the mastectomy and reconstruction took place as one event, so when I awakened from anesthesia, the deed was done. I knew very well what was at stake so my first words as I came to, thick with nausea, were: " and the lymph nodes?" A-OK. Thank goodness! So I went right back to sleep and stayed there for the next 15 hours.

The other remarkable thing about this hospital was that they embraced alternative healing practices. Not only did they allow a Reiki therapist to work on me just before surgery and then immediately after right in the recovery room, but they billed me for it through the hospital. I believe that this was one of the factors that helped me recover so quickly. It also gave me hope that things were changing in the field of Western medicine.

My plastic surgeon was (and is) extraordinary. She studied to be an artist until she decided to make a right turn into medicine, bringing her keen eye and delicate motor skills to the field of plastic surgery, with a specialty in breast reconstruction. Our appointments were all about how she would reshape my figure and construct the "seams" of my new topography. She showed me pictures and looked me straight in the eye when we talked. She answered dozens of questions with patience and keen intelligence. As it turned out, I healed beautifully and got the breast reduction and uplift I had secretly wanted for years. And now, over a decade later, I am free of cancer and healthier than ever. The unexpected bonus: she has become one of my closest friends.

I was oddly happy in the weeks leading up to my surgery. Instinctively, I knew that this respite was something I desperately needed. I was never afraid. Why? For once, I had given up control, and yet I sensed everything would work out. I was reassured that the cancer was very early stage, and I guess I just had faith. Oddly enough, it felt perfectly natural.

For this little workaholic, the change of pace was welcome when it came. My first couple of weeks of recovery at home were spent gently existing. Just BE-ing. For once in my life I didn't feel compelled to accomplish anything, except get better, which my body had to do on its own. No amount of forcing or cajoling would change the fact that I needed to rest, and it wasn't hard to do that. I was wiped out.

I am one of those people who doesn't tolerate anesthesia well. In fact, it kicks my butt. Every. Single. Time. It took me longer to recover from that than I expected. For the better part of a week, I was somewhat dazed and exhausted. While I was uncomfortable (my friends remind me, I would enter a room bent over in a pathetic posture protecting my injured chest), I managed the pain by taking only Extra Strength Tylenol and lying down for days. I cannot take anything stronger because I get severely nauseous and dizzy from painkillers. I didn't have the strength to read and had zero interest in TV. The most entertainment I required was listening to the birds chirping outside my bedroom window or warming myself in the sun outside on the deck.

I found the lack of stimulus to be very Zen. Hours drifted by and I noticed beautiful small things from my vantage point upstairs...the shadow of a bird's wing across my second-floor window, or the changing light patterns on the wall as the day went from morning to evening. These were subtleties that I missed as I rushed about my normal days. As most of us surely miss every day.

Medically, I was very lucky. The size, type and location of my cancer enabled me to get by with no further treatment—no chemo, no radiation and no drugs of any sort. To me, surgery is the easy part. To have any foreign substance in my body systemically would have been harder to deal with. This is why I say I was lucky in the scheme of things. Measuring all the losses I have endured, I am humbled by the knowledge that others have had it so much worse.

Once I started to feel better, I made small moves that changed my life in big ways. First, I had <u>lunch with friends</u>. During the day! Unless you've worked ten-hour days for twenty years, you don't know what a treat this is. People actually have a life between nine and five. I took leisurely strolls alone and reconnected with people who meant so much to me, but I'd only seen a handful of times in recent years because I was working all the time. (Today my life is rich with this type of socialization, so I know I've made the right choices.)

Second, I started to paint again. Just mixing colors and feeling the brushstrokes was tremendously healing. I admit my inner "alpha" got the better of me, and before my leave of absence was up, I painted a collection of work in anticipation of our opening the new gallery that we had just set up in our summer cottage in the Rocky Neck Art Colony, in Gloucester. All the paintings were imbued with uplifting messages and bright colors, expressing my newfound peace of mind and happiness. This was the beginning of a personal journey that marked my first departure from my identity as a fashion designer.

Third, when the doctor gave me the all-clear, I headed to the gym and hooked up with the best personal trainer I could hope for. I told her my condition, and she developed a Pilates routine for me to rebuild my strength and range of motion. She now has made it her protocol for recovering mastectomy clients, and we even got written up in Pilates Style magazine back in 2006. She has also become a close friend. That led me back to yoga, which is now an integral and essential part of my life.

People who know me well know I prefer to be happy no matter what. I work hard at it. I don't like to dwell on the negative. I try to find the silver lining in every case—and if not that, then I look for the lesson to be learned. This experience gave me plenty in that department. Lessons were everywhere, and it gave me so much to be thankful for.

Every situation offers plusses and minuses. In this case, the minuses were obvious. All the stress of medical procedures and the powerfully charged concept of cancer swept over me like a tsunami. And, I lost a part of my body. There's no doubt that's not one's first choice.

But, in the plus column:

— I learned very quickly who my true friends are—and there are many.

— I learned how to ask for help and not be ashamed to receive it.

— I gained two amazing new friends (my surgeon and trainer). I have such respect for these women who work hard and give so much.

— My priorities quickly shuffled into place. Things that used to be so important became less urgent and my health, my peace of mind, my family and friendships began to take top priority in my life.

No one goes through the experience of having cancer and emerges the same as they were before. In my case, it served to make me simultaneously stronger and more vulnerable. I am grateful for both.

Vulnerability taught me compassion. I learned to ask for help and was blessed to have it—my family and close friends were there for me—unobtrusively, thoughtfully and completely. Whenever I tell my story, I am reminded that my experience pales in comparison to others I have heard and witnessed.

Everyone's story is unique and personal, but there is a common thread of humanity that knits our experiences and makes us united. Those who survive often learn what it takes to thrive. Being a breast cancer survivor has become an essential part of the fabric of who I am.

Twelve years later, I can see how it was only the first of several life-changing upheavals that led me to where I am today…

Mysteries of Land and Sea

The Unraveling

"The way I see it, he said, you just can't win it.
Everybody's in it for their own gain. You can't please them all."
—Joni Mitchell

The signs were all there, though I didn't see them at first. As soon as I returned to the helm, after my medical leave, things seemed different. It may have been pure coincidence, but I felt as though the top execs at Liz Claiborne recognized my absence as an opportunity to prove I wasn't essential. I sensed I was being gently coaxed into a role of figurehead—the face of the brand—while someone else slid into place to call the shots.

During the nine years under the Liz Claiborne umbrella, we had six different presidents, all of whom I was required to report to. Change was constant, but while this was all happening, we had a fashion line to get out. I liken it to trying to fix your bike while you're riding it. It's hard to describe the complexity of producing a constant flow of high quality, well-merchandised, perfectly-timed, beautiful clothing. We had unleashed a machine that needed to be fed constantly and, at times, the sheer magnitude of the undertaking was overwhelming. As a design team, we had done this every year for many seasons, but never had to juggle the issues of a larger enterprise at the same time.

From the start, the hallmark of our original company was its organic, creative collaboration between all departments. I was determined not to lose this, the heart of what we had established. I knew we had big challenges ahead of us and believed that the best option was to continue working together in sync, with clear and open communication across all levels.

In a public corporation, however, it's all about hierarchy. I was new to this, and the chain of command confounded me. My president reported to a group president, who reported to the EVP, and the EVP reported to the CEO, who ultimately answered to the Board of Directors. We spent more time reporting "up" than guiding and inspiring the people who did all the work. It felt very counter-intuitive.

The word "synergy" began to take on a sinister connotation. It meant: anything that could be absorbed into LCI's existing operations would be eliminated. We had already seen too much of this. The first to go was our customer service and collections department. Since we had built our sales volume with a solid base of over 2000 small specialty stores, there was a heavy emphasis on connectivity—establishing positive personal relationships with our network of sales reps and with shop owners themselves.

Our company was an anomaly in the apparel industry. We "carried our own paper", which meant that our customer service staff called accounts to remind them that payment was due, and they paid us directly. Most companies do this through a third party called a "factor". But we started small, and even as we grew bigger, the lingering illusion of modest, personal scale was part of our charm. It allowed us to be over ninety percent current with our collections. The women assigned to do the customer calls knew the folks on the other end of the line, often asking about family events, weddings, grandchildren, etc., before proceeding to the reason for the call. While we valued the close-knit community we had formed, the expense was significant, contributing to the low profit margin that the corporation was intent on improving. So, we said goodbye to the first batch of devoted employees who had invested heart and soul into the company they revered.

And that was just the beginning...

· · ·

After that, we closed our distribution center and shipping was moved to LCI corporate centers in New Jersey. The boxes of merchandise that our accounts received no longer were packed in SIGRID OLSEN branded boxes. They were cheaper boxes, all sealed with Liz Claiborne tape. I don't know why, but this small detail really pissed me off.

Seated next to the corporate head of distribution at a dinner one night, I implored,

"Can we please use the SIGRID OLSEN logo on the boxes we ship to our accounts? Right now, they have Liz Claiborne tape on them and the stores find that very confusing. I thought the parent company was supposed to be invisible. Not only that, one store complained that their thirty-piece order arrived in eight different boxes. Does that make sense?"

I was quickly shut down. He gave me a shrug and said, "Sorry, Sigrid, but there's nothing I can do about that."

End of discussion. Each time something like this happened, it added to the heaviness building in my heart. But I was still optimistic that, with a convincing argument, some of the wrongs could be corrected. I was always looking for the bright side to emerge.

Even as more layoffs loomed, I tried to stay open to change. With the exit of the customer service staff and the increase of department store sales volume, our specialty store business began to flounder. It was decided that the commission-based independent sales reps, who were like family, and had been with us for several years, were too costly. They were replaced with Liz-trained, in-house sales staff, who had no idea the history and uniqueness of the business we'd built over the last two decades. It did not go well. Before long, the specialty stores sales dwindled, while the larger department store orders were on the rise. The top line grew larger and the bottom line (profit margin) soared as well. I was dismayed, but top management was jubilant.

I cannot describe how heart-wrenching it was to see the human toll that all these changes took on the people with whom I had worked in unison for most of my career. Around the office, there were days that were downright funereal. Our workload never diminished, so there was no time to pause and reflect on our loss. The grief was stuffed deep inside and festered there for several years.

We soldiered on, doing our best, and those who remained were determined to prove our excellence with unflagging determination. But we could feel it. The shining pinnacle we had always seen as our communal goal was elusive. We climbed and climbed, but never got to the summit. For many of my staff, it was unrelenting work with little personal satisfaction.

It became more and more difficult to maintain the upbeat, optimistic, creative atmosphere we had enjoyed for so many years. Many of my loyal staffers began to question their future. There were many departures, but none shocked me like the day Dorian stepped into my office and quietly announced she was leaving. Naively, I'd thought we'd be together forever, but I couldn't blame her. In some ways, I was even envious. After decades in the business, creating huge successes for other brands, she was finally being offered the opportunity to start her own line. My heart was broken, but I wished her well.

With all the layoffs mounting around us, several of my key design and production people followed, some joining her at her new venture and others fleeing for different opportunities.

No matter how prepared I thought I was, massive changes like this rocked me to the core. The earth was shifting beneath me, and I had the sense that more eruptions were in store.

As morale continued to decline, I just tried to do my job and not overthink. Unschooled as I was in the manipulative machinations of corporate hierarchy, it was hard to ignore the unspoken power struggle lurking beneath the surface. When the interference became intolerable, I would ask for a meeting with the CEO, or the EVP, second-in-command.

I clearly recall sitting down in each of their offices, exhausted and discouraged by the conflicting agendas coming at me from above—with a near-constant imposition of new people in charge of our brand. All the execs had always seemed like decent people to me, so I thought my point of view made perfect sense, as I appealed to their human side.

"I just want to do good work, design great clothes and be a good person. Is that so hard?" Seemed simple enough to me.

Instead of acknowledgement of the tough position I was in, I received a stream of corporate doublespeak about "synergies" and "change management" and was encouraged to be a better leader and present a more positive facade to my staff.

Again, my naivety caught me off-guard. I was literally being asked to be inauthentic, which, to me, was the worst possible betrayal to my brand and my company. I was willing to work long hours, persevering, striving, juggling multiple priorities, but I wasn't thrilled about compromising my integrity.

Things were complicated enough, but I soon learned that there was an even more nefarious initiative afoot, progressing without my input or knowledge. To this day, after inquiring with every top executive, all the way up to the CEO, I have no answer as to *why* SIGRID OLSEN was selected to be the guinea pig for a new design and production model that would revolutionize the way we did almost everything. (Oh, and by the way, it turned out to be an epic failure.)

A small team of operational geniuses at Liz had devised a brand new "fast fashion" prototype that would bring the design, merchandising and manufacturing teams together under one roof, close to the factories that produced our goods, which meant moving everything to Hong Kong. This required us to fire my entire fashion design and production team, many of whom had been with me for ten to fifteen years, replacing it with new people, located in Asia. They had already brought in a new design director who, while extremely talented himself, knew nothing about the unique heritage of our brand. This, coupled with a corporate mandate to increase profit margins, caused a shift in the quality and look of the clothes that was obvious to our customers.

I was so distressed by this news that I didn't sleep well for months. The emotional toll was bad enough—another case of being forced to part with key members of my design team, who had stuck with me through all the traumatic restructuring after the buyout. Logistically, it was problematic as well. Our home office in Wakefield, Massachusetts that, at its height, housed 150 employees, would be abandoned. Our current staff of 50-75 people would be reduced to twelve, mostly those who worked directly with me. The added obstacle of having to guide, manage and inspire a design team that was based halfway around the world, further complicated by a twelve-hour time difference, was nearly impossible to overcome.

At one point, the interpersonal dynamics got so hellish that we hired a corporate psychologist to come in to try and negotiate a truce. We had some pretty ugly sessions around the table, with no resolution. I remember writing in my journal after one of these roundtables, *"How can we be a feel-good brand when we don't feel good?"* No one was happy. Morale was at an all-time low. Even the people who proposed this initiative began to question its validity. But, like so many projects that I had witnessed while at LCI, this one had its own life force and there was no way to stop it. As it turned out, we didn't have to. Its lifespan ended when the company was ruined beyond recognition.

We had no choice but to work within the constraints of this new structure. They tried to appease me by giving me the lead role in finding, designing and setting up our new office space. I appreciated the gesture. At this point in my life I would have given anything to have a workplace more integrated with my lifestyle, less industrial and more personal. I had a few requirements: windows that opened to let in fresh air, plenty of natural light, and a real kitchen where we could all gather and eat home-cooked food. I also imagined an open, expansive floor plan, where we could feature all the products we made together in a unified brand showroom. By then we had licensees for handbags, jewelry, eyewear, bedding and bath decor. My vision was to allow all aspects of the design aesthetic to feed off each other and look cohesive.

We found our spot in a building that housed only two other companies, so it felt less formal, even though it was in a giant office park. I had hoped to find something more human-scaled, but that was nearly impossible. Nevertheless, it fit all my particular stipulations. It was an absurdly generous space—9,000 square feet for fifteen people—and there was plenty of room to hold regular design meetings with visitors from New York.

I am a big believer in visuals, so the walls were all outfitted with grids that could easily show outfits, samples, prints and concept boards in real time as we designed the collections. Everyone had ready access to this prominent display, keeping us all on the same page as we went about our work. We had a library nook with a comfy sofa, well stocked with design and art books for inspiration. It was a truly collaborative workspace.

The kitchen was equipped with a real stove (I fought for this, even though the office park developers thought I was nuts), because I am not a fan of microwave meals. Some days, we were lured by the aroma of freshly baked brownies or fragrant homemade soups. There was a full-sized refrigerator and massive wooden table, large enough for us all to sit together at lunch, like a family. If we were no longer the powerhouse organization we once were, I reasoned, at least we could take advantage of our small size by having a happy workplace. You would think all these creature comforts would interfere with productivity, but it was just the opposite. As a result of this fertile environment, our design output was prolific.

We occupied this space for the next couple of years, until the company was shuttered forever, despite the fact they had signed a ten-year lease. Since we were the last bastion of authenticity in the company, my diminished staff worked diligently to retain our integrity. The textile department was somehow spared from the global move and was housed here. Print design was the one thing that I could not let go of, since it was the reason I became a fashion designer in the first place. After some intense negotiation, they capitulated and allowed us to keep the print design process in our domain, while the rest of the design took place in the newly-outfitted Hong Kong office.

None of this came cheap. The cost of hiring and relocating designers (only one was already in Hong Kong) to the foreign office was steep, as were the various severance packages for those who were laid off. There were unfinished leases, upgrades in Hong Kong, and huge money spent on travel since, once launched, the design process required me and my latest president to be there to oversee everything at least once a quarter.

Despite our best attempts, it was not working. Every single time we showed up to review the work in progress, it was so far off that we scrambled to make it right, always racing against the clock, desperate to conjure up the magic that was lost in the move. We never did.

The first samples designed in Hong Kong arrived at the New York office just in time for our Spring 2007 market, and I hopped on a plane from Boston to see them for the first time. I arrived that morning before anyone else and ventured into the showroom to take a look.

To the unschooled eye, everything was in order and the product was adequate. But my well-trained sensibilities saw a hundred flaws—the colors were garish, some of the fabrics seemed cheap and the whole effect was inauthentic. It wasn't me. It was more like a clever copy than the real thing. I remember dashing into the bathroom to have a good cry. I had the sense that something significant was lost and would never be recovered. It was proof that if you mess with the process, it wreaks permanent damage on the product.

Even our beautiful New York showroom fell victim to corporate confusion. Things were constantly shifting so unpredictably, it was hard to understand who was in charge and what were our mutual goals. As overshadowed as I may have felt leading up to this time, it was nothing compared to what happened in the last months of our company's existence.

So many of our staff had been let go or relocated, we had extra floorspace on the 26th floor where our showroom was located, so Liz Claiborne started using our space for various overflow projects—for example, the outlet division needed a workroom, a finance group need a place to meet. As the weeks progressed, there were more and more unfamiliar faces.

It hit an all-time low for me one day when I arrived early on a flight from Boston for a day of meetings. I walked in and took a seat next to the reception desk, waiting for my first appointment of the day. I no longer had an office there, and it was odd having no spot on the entire floor to call my own, where I could put my briefcase and things for the day. As I sat, feeling completely displaced, I was faced with the ultimate disrespect, an ugly example of how much things had changed.

A young woman I had never seen before approached me and asked: "Excuse me, may ask your name? Who are you here to see?"

I'm thinking...you have *got* to be kidding. "I'm Sigrid," I said in a tentative voice, hardly believing that I was no longer recognized in my own showroom.

"Sigrid who?"

Oh. My. God. *"Sigrid Olsen,"* I replied, exasperated. "See, my name here on the door?"

"Oh. Okay," She said and turned on her heels, abruptly exiting the showroom.

I sat there, completely stunned, trying not to cry. I wondered: what the hell is happening here?

What happened to me that day probably had its roots in events that took place years before. I still look back and try to analyze exactly when I lost control of my name, my livelihood, my dream, but the answer isn't very clear. Was it just my agreeable nature that caused me to submit to the men in my company—first Peter and David, then Ed, and ultimately Liz's CEO?

I had grown up in this business and never felt marginalized because of my gender. I was surrounded by powerful women in high positions. But there were clues all along that I could have noticed had I been a more suspicious creature. Meetings held behind closed doors. Dilution of my stock to allow new shareholders to join the executive team. Increasing decisions being made without me. I was too busy being happy and creative in my design world. By the time 2007 arrived, my fate was clear. I was on my way to being the figurehead of an enterprise managed by people who thought they knew more about my company than I did.

All of this turmoil coincided with a widespread decline in the nation's economy. There was a massive retail consolidation happening, which had dire effects on the fashion industry. Major department stores, many of which were the cornerstones of our business, simply disappeared, swallowed up into larger entities. We lost Marshall Fields, Dayton Hudson, Parisian, May Company, just to name a few. By 2008, the situation worsened with colossal crises in banking and real estate as well.

Meanwhile, there was a changing of the guard at Liz Claiborne, Inc. Our current CEO was set to retire, and a new CEO was poised to take his place. At first glance, this seemed like a breath of fresh air. The incoming CEO was young and dapper, and seemed to be truly curious about what made each brand tick. I was sure he would understand how the fractured structure of this mega conglomerate needed retooling. After thoughtfully listening to each of our divisions about the direction we thought the corporation needed to take, he set about a massive reorganization.

We were all on pins and needles, waiting to hear the outcome: who would remain and whose division would be on the chopping block. I was aware that things weren't so good at my company. We'd had declining sales for a few quarters, and now were now grappling with this untenable global work-shift situation, but I was confident he would see the strength of our loyal following and the untapped power of the brand. We had 54 retail stores and were just about to sign a new license for furniture. Everything was bound to improve.

In July of 2007, the pronouncement was made. It came via email while I was in Richmond, Virginia, visiting a factory that would be making our newly-designed sofas and chairs. The deal was yet to be finalized, but I was thrilled with the prospect, simply in awe of all the possibilities for home furnishings that lay ahead.

To say I was shocked when I saw my name on the *strategic review* list would be an understatement. I felt like I had been punched in the stomach. What now? What did this even mean?

Strategic review was a term used to classify any division that would either be sold, kept, or closed down. There was a six-month period designated to pursue each of these options, at which time a final decision would be made. This was my first real encounter with failure, and I didn't like it, at all. I was determined to turn things around, but ultimately it was out of my hands. I could only hope now that we would find a buyer who would see the extraordinary niche my brand fulfilled and undo all the missteps that had caused us to flounder. It seemed like an easy fix to me.

The next few months were excruciating. Uncertainty is an affliction that seeps into your consciousness. We were unsure how to proceed. Designing nine months in advance, I had the sense that the concepts we were working on might never see the light of day. Some days, it seemed like we were all just going through the motions, with a tiny glimmer of hope that a buyer would come along and see how fabulous we were, like an orphan eagerly waiting for adoption. We needed a new family, and then everything would be better.

In New York, a team was assembled to broker sales of the various companies to prospective buyers. By this time, as our division was whittled away, we had the good fortune of keeping our best and final president. He was an expert at straddling the difficult chasm between following corporate mandates and appeasing the real people whose lives would be affected by the outcome of events. He always treated me with kindness and respect and appealed to my innate intelligence. We could discuss issues from both sides, and he understood the passion that fueled me, often talking me down when things got unbearable. He had a knack for understanding the human toll this situation was taking on all of us, living in a perpetual state of uncertainty. He, too, hoped that there was light at the end of this nightmarish tunnel.

There were so many moments when I felt close to giving up. I was ready to wash the bitter taste of betrayal out of my mouth and start fresh. But I hung on with my team to await the pronouncement of our collective destiny.

By the time I received the final phone call from the CEO, I was prepared. I'm often asked about that moment. How did it feel to get that fateful call? Honestly, it felt like *relief*. Months of torture were behind us. I already knew my life was about to change forever. I had carried a dark kernel of dread around with me for weeks, even months. Now, I was receiving the last word on the other end of the phone line.

"Hi, Sigrid, do you have a minute?"

Heavy pause. "Sure."

He blathered on a bit about the strain and uncertainty of the last six months and how they had examined how to save the business, or at least sell it, and had come to the only viable conclusion. Then, maybe, he threw a few compliments out, like how talented and dedicated my team and I had been, but all I remember is this:

"We have decided to close your business."

"Ok, thanks. Bye." is what I wanted to say. There was nothing more to discuss. I contained my anger and buried my shame, calmly asking a few logistical questions:

"How will we notify everyone about this?

"What happens to our office and all the contents?"

Lastly—"How long do we have?"

"You have until next Monday" was the reply. Just over a week.

Holy shit. Fourteen years of archives, nine thousand square feet of office space and twelve remaining staff were the physical remains of a company that was now being cast aside. We had ten days to get rid of everything. I felt sick. Hanging up the phone, I went back and sat down, totally stunned.

A tidal wave drenched me, but somewhere in the deepest part of the water, lay a gift. I could sense it, but not identify it. Its true significance would take months to really come to me.

In the crazy week that followed, we packed up years of memories and made a collective exit from a work life we loved, with people we cared about, and each set off to find the next step in our individual journeys.

Over time I have learned this: *Success is not always the best teacher. Failure makes you learn.* Once you know this, it's easier to accept disappointment and to use it as a life lesson.

I gained everything from the upheaval of this experience. It paved the way for positive changes that blossomed into the new life I have today. None of this would have evolved if I had not been forced to give up the one thing I thought I couldn't live without.

Clean Slate

"May all beings be peaceful.
May all beings be happy.
May all beings be safe.
May all beings awaken to the
Light of their true nature.
May all beings be filled with loving kindness."
—Buddhist Metta Prayer

After such immense upheaval, I sensed the need for an entirely new way of living. The frenetic pace of my life had come to an abrupt halt, but inside I felt my pulse racing like it always had. With nothing but time on my hands, I resumed my yoga practice, but even that didn't have the power to counteract my natural tendency towards *doing*. The Zen of *being* still hadn't quite sunk in yet. My mind continued to churn out ideas, and I filled my sketchbooks with plans for future businesses. It was time to break that pattern and try a new approach.

Instead of wallowing in self-pity or resentment over the loss of my company, I was determined to take this experience and use it to transform my life.

With all the distractions and pressures of my usual routine cleared away, I was now alone with myself, determined to get to know the real *me* again. It was as though I had been so preoccupied, I'd forgotten that the most important things in life are the most basic—peace, happiness, safety, and one's true self (not ego).

A couple of weeks after my business closed, I did something I had never done before. Enticed by my friend (and previous plastic surgeon) Bev's invitation for a girls' getaway, I joined her for a weekend at the famed Canyon Ranch Spa in Western Massachusetts. I was introduced there to the Buddhist Metta Prayer that starts this chapter. It was the first time I'd heard this prayer sequence, and its boundless simplicity struck a chord. In the thirty odd years I had spent on the outskirts of various mystical and spiritual teachings, I was surprised I had never run across it before. Immediately after class, I went up to my room and quickly logged onto my laptop to see what this sacred prayer was all about.

I learned that in Buddhist practice one repeats the lines five times, building on the theme of loving-kindness. Each recitation is directed at a different entity—first towards oneself, next towards a loved one, then a stranger, then an enemy (usually the tricky one) and finally towards all beings. I'm not a practicing Buddhist, but something in the ritual felt expansive to me. It was as if the positive energy would keep growing and permeate all the different parts of my life.

I also understood it as a way to develop compassion and forgiveness—something I needed at a time when I could have done just the opposite. I copied the words into my journal and peeked at them occasionally in the weeks to come. Whenever my busy brain started to feel jagged and out of control, the rhythm of these phrases made it feel smooth again.

This meditation on love became the foundation for my awakening. As I stumbled through the ups and downs of those first few months of unemployment, I used it as a touchstone. I was untethered, and it felt strange. Circling back to this simple teaching helped keep me on course, aligned with something greater than myself. It helped me believe in the power of love to transcend my attachment to the life I used to have.

The trip to Canyon Ranch was an act of uncharacteristic generosity toward myself. It wasn't a destination on my must-visit list. It had always seemed too grand, too self-indulgent, the time and the expense an extravagance I had never allowed myself to consider. When Bev asked if I would join her for a long weekend there, I almost said no (out of habit). But then after a brief internal squabble, my usual pragmatic *don't-you-have-something-more-important-to-do* reflex fortunately lost out to my newly unleashed *what-the-hell-why-not* adventurous spirit.

So, on a snowy January morning, I loaded my yoga mat and small bag of clothes into the back of Bev's Audi TT, and we set off to Lenox, Massachusetts for a weekend of healthy girl time. I was feeling a bit shy at first because we didn't know each other all that well. Our budding friendship just needed a little time to germinate, I thought, and it would end up being important to both of us. I was right, our affinity became clear after just a few hours together, and we developed a playful, but respectful, sisterly bond.

We had met three years before when she performed the breast reconstruction surgery after my mastectomy. A very busy and successful doctor, she was gracious and kind when I needed it, and we became friends. We discovered many shared traits—we were both strong, independent, professional women at a crossroads. My life intersection was more urgent and certainly more apparent than hers, but we had each reached a point in our lives where we were questioning things and looking for something more than all of our achievements had produced. Now that we were in our fifties, we yearned for self-knowledge and serenity, knowing instinctively that making a mind-body connection was the path to getting there.

Snowflakes swirled around us as we made our way west on Route 2 through central Massachusetts. During the three-hour drive, we exchanged backstories. As women, we naturally have a way of relaxing into who we really are, once we let down our guard and give up our need to appear in control. Vulnerability opens up the space for real friendship and intimacy. So, I told Bev all about what it had felt like deconstructing my business and closing the book on that chapter of my life.

"It was so *odd*," I mused. "This past week has been like an out-of-body experience, where I am watching myself go through the motions—cleaning out my desk, packing up everything, saying goodbye, shutting down my e mail—essentially exiting my role as SIGRID OLSEN. Now, I wonder who I am going to *be* once I let go of the person I *was*. I'm so identified with my career that it's going to take some work to sort through all the deeply ingrained self-importance to get back in touch with my real self. That's okay. My calendar is blank, and I guess I have nothing better to do." I gave her a sardonic smile. "It's strange not to be in demand anymore. No calls. No emails. No one lining up outside my office door waiting for my opinion. Is this what failure feels like?"

She caught me as I was falling, not allowing me to succumb to self-pity. "Sigrid, you are the most industrious and self-motivated person I know. You will be just fine. The collapse of your business takes you outside your comfort zone. Look at it as an opportunity to reinvent yourself and apply your talents in a whole new way. Starting fresh can be a great thing. I know you well enough to be sure you'll make the most of it."

I had already taken steps to start the New Year with a clean slate, literally. I told her about the nutritional cleanse I started with a group at my gym just a couple of weeks before. When my good friend and trainer P.J. asked if I wanted to join her and a few others on a modified fast, to break in the New Year I thought, "Why not?"

It had been a really hard six months. I was feeling lost and therefore open to anything. Deep in the trenches of self-doubt, I was drained from trying to understand what had happened to my company and exhausted from the months of passive waiting for the final word to come down from the executive offices at Liz Claiborne. I wondered if I could manage to commit to anything, but I did. I just said yes and immersed myself in the intensive and strict program.

I had done my share of fasting and experimentation over the years, but it had been a while since I'd given my health that much attention. Nothing was stopping me now. No meetings, business trips or fancy dinners to distract me—I was free to focus on purifying, mentally and physically. The regimen gave me a sense of control over *something* in my life. It also provided a goal. I dove in, and it was the perfect thing at the perfect time.

Bev was right, I had the inner strength to get through this transition and the change might turn out to be just what I needed.

I made a conscious choice to let go of the old habits and thought patterns that inhibited me. I stepped off the *go-go-go* treadmill of my former life and tried to relax into a new rhythm.

The very pared down diet left me slightly hungry all the time and somewhat high, giving me a sense of detached calm. I felt peaceful and centered. Looking in the mirror I saw bright blue eyes looking back at me with intense clarity. Wow! I was surprised to admit I felt happy, even light-hearted.

At a time when my life appeared to be falling apart, I was filled with gratitude, instead of regret. Hard as it was, there was a certain lightness of spirit that accompanied the heartache of losing my company. Maybe I was delirious from malnourishment or endowed with some sort of fleeting clairvoyance, but I had an inkling that there was a new reality awaiting me that might prove to be more fulfilling than anything I had ever experienced.

Telling Bev about the effects of my new diet, I was keenly aware that, as a physician, she might be skeptical. "Two weeks have passed since I started this cleanse and, I have to admit, I feel pretty great. It's a twenty-one-day regimen of eating only certain foods, mostly fruits and vegetables, and three days controlled fasting. I'm on Day 12 now, eating mostly green vegetables, apples and pears, and I swear it has kept me sane and energized when part of me has just wanted to sit on the couch and eat Haagen-Dazs."

She glanced over at me, eyebrows lifted, waiting for me to go on. She seemed genuinely interested, so I continued, "To be honest, I've had to be strong for everyone else, but it has been months of torture. I nearly lost it a couple of times. And the worst part? The *uncertainty*. I *hate* not knowing what to strive for. I've been working towards this one goal for most of my adult life. It's so disorienting to be changing focus midstream. But now, after just a couple of weeks of distance and cleansing, the way I feel gives me incentive to keep going, to try to form a whole new kind of life."

As we drove, I began to open up more and was candid about the toll the last six months had taken on my psyche. It felt good to be able to process my feelings with an objective listener.

"The hardest part of all of this, emotionally, is the human loss. I can deal with the fact that my dream didn't turn out the way I expected. Losing my company definitely sucks. But I'll find a new path. It's the lasting friendships I can't replace. We were like family, and little by little, we have been torn apart and made to go our separate ways. At one time, our local office held 150 people. By last year, we dwindled to twelve. For those of us who remained, the harder we got pushed, the stronger we became. We felt so lucky. It was incredible, a life woven together of creative collective purpose, and now, it's all unraveled."

I realized, as I said this, that even if I could shed a positive light on the ordeal for myself, my coworkers were coping with their own trauma over the closing. "It wasn't just me who suffered. Some of my staff had been with the company fifteen years and thought they'd be there fifteen more. Many people were angry. Some were terrified. Most of us were just sad."

It was quiet in the car for the next few minutes, Bev taking in everything, while I was lost in thought. I was grateful to be traveling with a friend who understood from her own experience what it meant to build a business from scratch and create a workplace that held one's essence within its walls. She continued to listen as I recounted the story of my last days at the helm of SIGRID OLSEN.

"We were given just one week to clear out the offices, sifting through twenty years of memories, deciding what to keep and what to let go of. The whole process felt very symbolic. Going through hundreds of photographs—pictures from sales meetings, company parties, award ceremonies and fashion shoots—reminded me of all the amazing people I'd met and worked with. Looking through piles of artwork that I'd created, prints we'd developed, sketchbooks filled with thumbnails of hundreds of collections from over two decades. It was overwhelming."

I could sense the compassion in Bev's voice as she asked, "How are you feeling right now?"

"Drained, but like a weight has been lifted. It was actually a *relief* when we got word it was over. At least now we could stop wondering and get on with our lives. It was heart-breaking but also freeing, like painting over an old canvas with white gesso and starting over. A clean slate. It's so weird to be doing this cleanse right now. Cleaning out my office and my body at the same time. The irony's not lost on me."

It was already dark that evening when we arrived at Canyon Ranch, and the surrounding landscape was draped with a soft blanket of new snow. We unloaded the car and checked in at the front desk just before dinner.

I was a little surprised at the facility, which seemed opulent and very traditional. I don't know what I was expecting—something more down to earth, more Zen. It looked like a beautiful, elegant, old world hotel—expansive lobby, uniformed staff, impressive modern art on the walls and in the corridors. Even our guest room was quite posh—poufy beds with soft cotton sheets, overstuffed chairs, damask upholstery, heavily curtained windows overlooking hundreds of acres that surrounded the sprawling mansion.

At first, I was disappointed not to be roughing it, but before long, I succumbed to the plush coziness, feeling almost giddy to be there.

After the drive, we were both a little bit dazed. We had talked so much we were drained of words, gladly surrendering to the stillness invoked by the retreat-like atmosphere of the spa. Neither of us could believe we were treating ourselves to this unexpected getaway and we looked forward to having plenty of time to do

whatever we wanted with hundreds of activities to choose from—
and *all* of them were *good* for us. I shook my head and smiled.

"This could be amazing. I'm so happy to be here."

I was especially grateful to be there with Bev, partly because
she needed the same healing I sought—unwinding from a stressful
job. But more so because she was not from my world. Her orbit
took her to hospital OR's and medical conferences—healing
people, even saving lives—far away from the superficiality of
fashion. I needed some distance. I had been immersed so deeply in
the apparel business, it had seeped into my cells. I was keenly
aware that it was time for me to purify, flush it all out and start
over.

On my first day at the spa, I woke before daybreak. Taking a
few moments to write in my journal, I hurried downstairs to join
the sunrise yoga session where I first was introduced to the
Buddhist Metta prayer. The heart of the class centered on
beginning the day with *Surya Namaskar*, the Sun Salutation,
repeating the sequence of poses several times. It was a great way to
wake up. My tired, stressed-out muscles struggled to keep up, but
at the end, after *Savasana* (the all-important resting pose), I was
rejuvenated. It felt good to surrender to the flow, my body having
memorized it thirty years ago when I first started yoga.

*This five-thousand-year-old ritual was
imprinted on a primal part of me that had been
locked away for years, waiting to be unleashed
again. Now, I was bowing and stretching,
loosening limbs that had spent too long sitting at
a desk, and slowly the knots of tension began to*

dissolve. A seed of hope sprung in my heart and I promised myself I would tend to it with loving care.

After class, I joined Bev in the cafe just as she was finishing up her breakfast. Still engrossed in dietary re-entry after the cleanse, I opted for a cup of green tea and a bowl of yogurt with berries, and even that seemed like a lot. Once I saw the list of activities that I was hoping to fit into our short stay there, I knew I would need nourishment. Bev and I studied the spa menu together, trying to plan just the right balance of exertion and indulgence. I chose a hot stone massage to finish the day and decided to try a special life-coaching workshop called "Mind Mapping," followed by a Pilates session and another yoga class. I wasn't sure if I would get through all the classes. I hadn't worked out like this in a while. I hoped I wouldn't embarrass myself by giving out halfway through a session. I listened while Bev ordered another latte and recited her day's agenda.

"I've set aside most of the afternoon for a whole-body seaweed treatment and deep tissue massage. I'm going to need it because look at my morning." She showed me the list of kick-ass workouts she'd scheduled for the few hours before and after her pampering. She was living it to the max, and I admired her for it. This woman was going to make every second count. My type-A side wanted to emulate her energy and discipline, but I knew that today my work was more about taking it down a notch—learning to relax.

The Mind Mapping workshop seemed like the perfect opportunity to address my current existential blank canvas. It was described as *"a practical and exciting take-home tool for identifying needs, dreams and new possibilities"* and, best of all, it offered a chance to draw. We would literally be mapping out a new course of action with this *"creative whole brain technique."* It seemed a bit pricey—$150 for less than an hour—but I thought it would do me good. At the very least, I would learn something.

When I walked into the conference room and saw the broken stubs of crayons on the table, my expectations immediately dropped, and my internal critic went into high gear. If I was going to draw, they could at least provide decent art supplies. I was already disappointed in the sterile surroundings, having thought we would have a studio space that would in itself inspire me.

What a rarified world I had gotten used to! My expectations were so high—I was spoiled and overly critical from all the years spent in a highly competitive, style-driven world. But even during those years, when I'd joined the execs on a corporate off-site, I'd always preferred natural light to the windowless air-conditioned rooms, where meetings were usually held.

I was intrigued by the Life Mapping concept, but I found this setup artistically uninspiring. As it turned out it wasn't about art at all.

There were four of us in the group, and I was the last to arrive. As I quietly slipped into a chair and listened to the leader welcome us and explain the theme of the workshop, I tried to keep an open mind.

"The purpose of this session is to enable you to get in touch with your unlocked potential and help you identify what's next for you in your life. Mind Mapping is an amazingly versatile tool to guide this process. Our minds are constantly churning with ideas and this technique helps capture all the rapid bursts of creativity that usually go unrecognized. The first step is to decide on a focal word (a central idea or thought) you want to explore. Don't think too hard; just write it down in the center of your paper. Then draw a circle around it."

I wrote the word *happiness* and circled it decisively. *The center of my sun.*

"OK now it's time to *branch out.* This means you will spontaneously connect any new words that come to you to the circled word and then add sub-branches to those words. Keep going until you have run out of words that connect to your original theme or its branches. Make sure you think creatively and intuitively—no editing. Your map will end up looking like a sketchy sun with multiple branches of rays that spread out to all corners of your paper. Circle the words that resonate the most strongly for you."

Diligently, I scribbled words and branches, stopping now and then to rake through my psyche for buried thoughts until I had filled the page. On my own, I used the crayon stubs to draw a sun on the paper, surrounded by the words I felt were the most important.

nature | creativity | beauty | spirituality |
simplicity | balance | inspiration

After about fifteen minutes she said, "Okay, now let's interpret our maps and see what they tell us."

The first thing I wrote down was:

- *Beauty is important to me.*

Followed by:

- *I want to spend much of my life outdoors, close to nature.*

Inspired, I kept writing, revisiting my heart for the truth, whenever my thoughts were stalled:

- *Creativity brings energy into my life.*
- *I can simplify and live with less.*
- *My focus must include balance and breathing.*
- *I must cultivate love in every part of my life.*
- *Worry interrupts my growth and enjoyment.*
- *It's harder to "dance through the day" when I am focused on the future.*
- *Greater clarity will come with greater simplicity.*
- *Vibrant health is important to me.*

Just as I was getting into it, the leader interrupted to provide the final question.

She said, "Ask yourself—*given all this, where do I go from here?*"

"Where do I go from here? Good question," I thought. "What had I learned?" I jotted down what came to me (in bullet points…my favorite listing technique):

- *Trust my instincts.*
- *Be myself.*
- *Let go of fears.*
- *Keep it simple.*

Then the class was over. Fifty minutes went by in a flash. I looked around. Was everyone else as startled as I was? Did they seem finished? Unsettling as it was to have been stopped so abruptly, I vowed to continue this process on my own and try to distill my life vision into a few simple ideas I could then put into practice. The short session certainly kick-started a new thought pattern, sparking new intentions informed by self-reflection. It was worth every penny. The morning's exercise had shown me the path ahead of me was clear. Wellness would be my top priority, and everything else would have to support that.

Bev and I met for a late lunch and exchanged reports about our day's activities. She had been to a series of challenging workouts, while I had focused more on internal calisthenics. I told her a little about my life-mapping exercise and realized in the recounting that although I was critiquing the session, it opened my eyes to an interesting process, one I was hoping to explore further.

"I have to admit," I said, trying to be fair and honest at the same time. "It was thought provoking. The workshop itself felt way too short, but it did spark something for each of us in the group. Everyone there was at a crossroads of some sort, looking for direction. I wish it had been longer. This is heavy stuff, and we barely scratched the surface."

The seed was planted. At the time, I never expected to create my own workshops, nor did I consider myself qualified to lead others on this type of journey. But, as it turned out, my experience at Canyon Ranch deeply affected me. The ideas that took root that weekend germinated over time and helped nourish the expanded "life-visioning" curriculum of the Creative Wellbeing Retreats that became part of the map of my future. Once I began to plan them for real, I made sure I provided top-notch art supplies—no broken crayons for me. I also chose dazzling natural environments, for participants to dream and play in.

Just like the Mapping episode, the entire weekend was too short. Bev and I reluctantly packed up our things on Sunday afternoon and headed back to our respective lives, recharged and thoughtful about our experience at Canyon Ranch. We were both committed to a healthy lifestyle, and it was understood that we would continue to support one another in our efforts to progress with our inner awakening. We had established our friendship on new ground. It wasn't based on outward trappings of success or status, but a shared personal journey. The weekend ignited in each of us a new appreciation for the richness life has to offer.

I returned home from this eye-opening trip with all good intentions to apply my happiness essentials, but before long, I was back to my usual routine—waking early each day, drinking tea on the puffy cream-colored couch in the living room, wrapped in a blanket, while a fire warmed the room. I was still caught up in trying to make *something* happen—scheming my next enterprise, trying to coax my life vision into reality. Notebook in hand, I journaled, keeping track of my prospects—starting multiple, simultaneous, ambitious projects that required online research, all in an attempt to determine my next incarnation. I even fielded a few unsavory calls from opportunistic venture capitalists, who hoped to take advantage of the brand's demise. Although I was tempted, I avoided falling into the trap of repeating past mistakes. But without the use of my name, the opportunities weren't viable anyway.

Trying to envision (translation: control) my future was like having my tarot read. I was putting my proverbial cards on the table, hoping that someone else would tell me what was around the corner. I knew my destiny was out there, but I had to learn how to interpret the reading.

What I came to realize was that this orientation towards wellness and self-knowledge was an entirely new message for me. It was time to stop striving. Time to look inward, take an unvarnished personal inventory and make some changes. If anything important was going to unfold, I couldn't expect it to be

~ 201 ~

brought to me. I had to create from the source, and that source was inside *me*.

The problem was that I was still deeply invested in my ability to *produce*. I had equated my personal success with how much I could accomplish, and the evidence of this was all around me. Every time I created anything at all in my studio, it immediately spiraled in my mind into a new, successful enterprise that would be just what I needed. My fantasy almost always positioned me in the perfect business—one that provided just enough money, but was also *super* creative, groundbreaking and life affirming.

I pictured myself in various idyllic workplaces—well-designed spaces with high ceilings, plenty of windows and easy access to the outdoors. *My* make-believe office would *not* be dependent on air-conditioning and fluorescent lights. We could open the windows! We could hear the birds! We would listen to great music! There would be a simple but attractive kitchen, stocked with healthy ingredients and an endless supply of spring water and green tea. People who worked there would be happy, cooperative, and healthy, not *stressed*. Best of all: *nobody would tell me what to do*.

Even as I write these words, they make me laugh because that's exactly what I got. Just on a much smaller scale than I imagined. My workplace is in my home. All the wished-for elements are there—the natural surroundings, expansive windows, open kitchen, access to a beautiful backyard with palm trees and a water view, even a small staff of happy workers, and one of them is me. Yet, I always want more. It's a curse.

*The internal contest between my compulsive desire to do and my enlightened instinct to let myself **be**, remains unresolved. This restlessness* *causes me to constantly re-imagine what can **be**, instead of allowing me to be satisfied with what **is**.*

One time, on vacation, I came across a fable I liked so much I made a plaque out of it and placed it in our guest bathroom for all to see.

It went something like this:

One day, while on vacation on a Caribbean island, an American businessman came upon a local fisherman sitting on the pier with a generous catch piling up beside him. He was impressed and stopped to congratulate the man on his bountiful haul.

"You're pretty good at this. Do you have your own boat?"

"Nope."

"You should get your own boat and hire a crew."

"Why would I want to do that?"

"Well, because then you'd catch even more fish."

"Why would I want to do that?"

"Because if you caught more fish, you would make more money."

"Why would I want to do that?"

"Because then you'd be rich and you could let everyone else work and you could just relax somewhere beautiful.

"You mean like I'm doing right now?"

I see myself in this story. As much as I want to identify with the wise fisherman, it's the clueless businessman, always wanting more, who I resemble. Why do I always have to complicate things? Why can't I just relax and enjoy the present moment? Why can't I be thankful for what I have? These frustrating questions represent a recurring theme in my life—a conundrum I have yet to solve, but I'm getting closer. That's why I look for ways to wipe the slate clean and begin anew. Every yoga class, body cleanse and immersion in nature is an attempt to start fresh and recapture my essence.

I realize, however, that my restless ambition also has a healthy side. It compels me to *keep trying*. My creative compulsion is indelibly written on my DNA. The continuous desire for a sense of purpose is a natural aspect of human nature, especially mine. This proactive energy is as much the key to my reinvention as it was to my success in business. The challenge for me is to be consistently mindful and balanced as I continue along my path. Slow down, *breathe* and *keep breathing*. When I do this, I actually accomplish more and damage myself less.

I learned a couple of very important lessons as a result of the mind-mapping and the cleansing process.

One: body, mind and spirit are indeed tied together. The purifying effects of my streamlined diet and emphasis on daily yoga and meditation had tangible results. The correlation between the purification of my physical self and the clarity of my thoughts became obvious. Emotions lost the power to sway me so profoundly and I felt more centered, able to trust my instincts once again.

Two: My need to succeed had become an impediment, a burden. I had to forge a completely new path. I had veered so far off the basic tenets which had guided me through the personal growth of my younger years, that small adjustments were no longer enough. My life needed a complete overhaul.

It was time to deconstruct the designer persona I had tenaciously built over the past several years and throw off the cloak of ego that had grown heavy, concealing the real me.

The solution was simple, but also the hardest thing in the world. I had to learn to learn to just *be*. This revelation is aptly described in one of my favorite quotes by Pierre Teilhard:

"We are not human beings having a spiritual experience. We are spiritual beings having a human experience."

The cleanse was so timely. For the better part of a year, poisonous thoughts and feelings had occupied my mind and spirit. Fear and self-doubt plagued me, and I was a roiling mess of conflicting emotions. Anger haunted me as never before. The feeling of unease would surely have evolved into *disease* if I hadn't done something.

Once I made a commitment to healing and reinvention, it was as though I'd leapt off a cliff into a benevolent, unknown territory. I've said many times that I would never have even peered over the edge, if I hadn't been forced to. I would have continued on my career path with unflagging determination. When that path became a major highway and then abruptly ended, I found it nearly impossible to take my foot off the gas. I thought, "Let me just slow down a bit. I've been driving way too fast." Really, what I needed to do was stop, park the car and get out and walk.

As time passes, I am increasingly grateful I have had the chance to rethink things. At some point in our lives, most of us wish to start over. Sometimes, the most powerful and life-changing events are unexpected, as they were in my case. But all the little, beautiful miracles that quietly awaited me were there all along. Unfortunately, I had been rushing by at breakneck speed and hardly noticed them.

The journey is not always easy, but it is consistently reaffirming. For a person who has always powered through life, always pushing to progress forward, trusting stillness is a constant challenge.

As I experience a deeper sense of serenity and satisfaction, I find the disruption of stress and anxiety intolerable. My happiness is measured in reverse proportion to the amount of anxiety I experience. Harmony and happiness are always there. I just have to get out of my own way.

I still keep the *Metta Prayer* close to my heart, invoking the wisdom of the words:

> *May I be peaceful. May I be happy. And most of all…May I awaken to the light of my true nature.*

Without that insight, I know my second act would inevitably be nothing but an empty replica of my first.

~ 207 ~

~ 208 ~

Escape Artist

*"For those who have an intense urge for spirit
and wisdom, it sits near them, waiting."*
—Patanjali (from the yoga sutras of Patanjali)

The winter was bleak when my company and I parted ways. With
all the packing and goodbyes at the office, January went by in a
blur. At home, after my brief excursion to Canyon Ranch, I was
back to a routine that had no real purpose—days that held no
promise. My mood matched the weather outside, which was grey
and chilly, and an icy emptiness seeped into my soul. As I tried in
vain to settle down and quiet my restlessness, I recalled the words
of wisdom my attorney told me as I prepared to negotiate the exit
of my contract during the last months at Liz Claiborne.

"Sometimes, a field has to go fallow for a while to be able to
produce crops."

I should have taken her advice to heart. Despite her impressive,
worldwide fashion expertise and offbeat designer attire, she was a
native Midwesterner with down-to-earth insights. She had a small,
but very hip, New York office in Soho and a penchant for diet
cola. This gave her an unusual demeanor; a wiry bundle of energy
in *Comme Des Garcons*, dispensing common sense at ninety miles
an hour. I ended up using her more for psychological than legal
counsel and relied on her to lift me up when I was feeling down.

The main thrust of her encouragement was to urge me to think deeply about my *hierarchy of values*. What was important to me? Money? Status? Freedom? I was so used to my jetsetter lifestyle and executive benefits, I was almost afraid to look the question straight in the eye. I knew I hadn't been happy for a while. My soul felt like it had been locked away and was aching to be set free. Was it possible that this might prove to be the perfect opportunity to live the authentic life I had been craving?

Funny that the most perceptive comments on my situation came from my attorney, but I began to seriously contemplate her query. She helped me understand that the essence of my brand was still part of me, and I could coax it into a new incarnation if I had faith and patience. Even though I knew her personal tastes ran more to the avant-garde, she seemed to have a remarkable understanding and appreciation for my design style. Since I had come to her dejected and exhausted from the struggle of maintaining my dignity in the face of corporate rejection, it felt good to have someone (anyone) in the industry give me positive feedback.

She used to say to me, "If I close my eyes and think of you, there is a supernatural *hum*. You are the Martha (Stewart) that we might want to have over for dinner." I was bolstered by her encouragement, but honestly, I suspect that the source of the hum she was talking about might have been a result of the cases of diet soda she had stockpiled in her office. Still...her words gave me hope and I wish I had heeded them sooner.

By mid-February, I was ready for a change of scenery. I had pondered my situation long enough and still sought something to quiet my restlessness. I needed to *escape* in the very best sense of the word. At home, I tended to obsess about what to do next, how to combat my feelings of loss and why this had all happened in the first place. Every morning, I got up and "went to work" which meant bundling up in front of the fireplace with a cup of tea and a sketchbook, writing notes to nobody and planning projects without an audience.

The faucet of my idea flow wouldn't turn off, and my metaphorical cup was overflowing. My biggest fear was that no one would have a need for my creativity ever again.

Every winter, Curtis and I vacationed somewhere warm and tropical, but we'd always had limited time and a strict schedule. Now, the future was open-ended. The fact that no one needed me was both disturbing and freeing. So, we prepared to head to Mexico for a dose of sun to cheer my spirit and warm our bones.

In keeping with the theme of freedom and flexibility, we each packed a small bag and, for the first time in twenty years, boarded a plane with no agenda in place.

Our destination, Tulum, two hours south of Cancun, was familiar to us as we had spent many vacations on the coast between there and the small island of Isla Mujeres, where we were married. The first time we visited Tulum, we were charmed. The unique beauty of the setting revolves around a long expanse of unspoiled beach, dotted with small hotels and casitas perched right on the sand. We felt right at home among retreat-goers, off-the-grid-vacationers, and *escape artists* such as myself.

On the approach to Cancun airport, I peered out my airplane window dazzled by the aquamarine waters below. I felt both wistful and excited. This was a different kind of trip for me, perhaps foretelling a completely new way of life—one that didn't involve five-star hotels and an expense account. It would be simple, no frills, and required nothing more than a willingness to live in the moment.

In the past, living in the moment wasn't an option. I was used to working nine to twelve months ahead of time. I also never took a vacation in February. For over two decades, February had meant only one thing: Spring Fashion. Normally, I would be sketching ideas for next year's collections and leafing through the pages of *Vogue* and *Elle* to get a glimpse of the current spring ad campaigns. My flight destination would have been Paris for the *Premiere Visione* Fabric Fair, and then on to London to meet with print studios and do a little shopping.

Instead, I was sitting on a plane to Mexico, wrestling with mixed emotions. While my colleagues were headed off to Europe, like a herd of black-clad chic sheep, I was headed for the Yucatan with a carry-on bag containing a pair of flip-flops, a swimsuit, some shorts, tees and a couple of *pareos*.

As soon as we landed in Cancun, the feel of the air in the jet-way was a sensual reminder of where I was going. I emerged from the terminal into the startling heat of the Mexican sun, feeling a bit adrift, yet hungry for something deeper to experience. I hoped that my escape was more than simply putting distance between me and a cold New England winter. I wanted it to usher me towards something truly amazing.

I knew instinctively this was an important juncture. My life was a blank slate, and I could do anything I chose, so I'd better choose wisely. After years of being responsible for so many others, this freedom felt disconcerting at first. But I took a deep breath, and then another one.

As layers of stress started to melt away, my soul began to come alive. The future stretched out ahead of me like so many miles of white sand beach—my thoughts the only footprints.

We didn't come to Tulum by accident. This part of Mexico was a mecca for spiritual seekers and vacationers looking for something more than a pool and a margarita. The Mayan ruins are nearby, and the entire beach is populated with people doing yoga poses facing the sea or sitting in meditation on the sand.

The beauty of seeing someone perform a truly graceful sun salutation, backlit by the sun rising over a sparkling sea is like starting the day at the ballet. The feel of the sand beneath my feet grounded me, and the spaciousness above gave me room to breathe. I started to really feel good. My heart expanded, and the fatigue and worry started to fall away.

They say the Mayans settled there because the east-facing coast generates power and that seems plausible to me. Feeling the vitality of the incessant wind is like plugging into an electrical socket—it's so energizing. Every morning a breathtaking sunrise makes getting up at dawn a ceremonious event. I knew from past trips to Tulum that, in a few days, I would adjust to a rhythm prescribed by nature. Wake up at dawn. Walk the glistening shoreline. Breathe. Eat lightly. Sleep deeply. Frolic in the waves. Close the day with yoga. Eat. Sleep. Repeat. Maybe I would learn patience after all.

Curtis and I were like nomads, exploring the coast with minimum possessions and no particular place to be. It was odd to travel without hotel reservations, but it allowed us to move about freely, trying various accommodations without concern about changing our minds. During the few weeks we were in Tulum, we stayed in six different places, with a wide range of accommodations.

The first night we checked into Maya Tulum, a well-known yoga hotel where we had stayed many times before. As we wound our way down the sandy path to our casita, I took note of the quiet, which settled gently in my heart, regretting every worry that ever consumed me. It all felt like a waste of precious time. I made a silent vow to be good to myself, let go of my fears and savor the simplest things.

That first evening as I dipped my tired, sandy feet into the ceramic foot-bath outside the yoga studio, I took pleasure in the beautiful simplicity of that act. Entering the domed circle of the studio, I felt immediately comforted by the prospect of practicing asanas in the golden light of the setting sun. I rolled out my mat and let my body and mind surrender, thankful I was smart enough to get myself there. It was just what I needed.

Being at Maya Tulum meant there was a yoga class to attend every day, sometimes twice a day. My body had learned these poses decades ago, while I was in my twenties, so once we got settled, I immersed myself naturally, forgetting I was thirty years older now. My hamstrings and my back remembered though!

Before long, I realized I had once again pushed myself too far, and I had to give myself a bit of a break. Lesson learned: don't bring your Type-A personality into the yoga room. I eased up on the strenuous yoga and continued soothing my soul and wounded ego with Mayan clay body wraps, hot stone massage and blissful immersion in the sights and sounds of seaside living.

Day by day, I felt myself unwind. As I walked the beach, I pondered my future conjuring up various scenarios of how I would go on now that the confines of my former life had been removed. It was good to have the time to talk freely with my husband about how we would adapt to this change of lifestyle and make the most of it.

One evening I meandered alone on the beach in the fading light, tracing the silver edge of the waves with my bare feet. The rhythm of the surf was reflected in the sound of my own breathing. Suddenly, everything seemed simple—proof of how the force of nature heals wounds.

It was as though the power of the relentless wind and the vitality of the sea simply washed away the complicated thoughts cluttering my brain. Suddenly, I was grateful for everything that had happened. Maybe I was finally learning not to push things and just *be*.

With everything stripped away and nothing but time on my hands, I was able to truly question everything.

It was great to be on vacation in Mexico, but honestly, it's not required. I know now that it just takes practice to look at life objectively, and you can do it anywhere.

Forget all the trappings of who you think you are, what others expect of you and relax into who you *really are*. Once you choose to take the path of wellness—getting healthy in both body and mind—the important thing is to identify what makes you happy and let go of the habits, people, and obligations that don't.

For me, it took getting away from my daily routine to see myself clearly. Here I had to answer to no one. I began to see my desire to please everyone—my family, friends, employees, customers and bosses—as a hopeless energy drain. I needed to recharge—replenish my reserves—and that was the intention of my escape.

I lived each day with relaxed clarity. Yoga helped with that. Learning to breathe deeply settled my jangling nerves in an instant. Over-achiever that I was, I still got a little antsy at the end of a day of doing "nothing", so at dusk I usually pulled out my art supplies and played with pen and color until I was satisfied. Afterwards, we would walk the shoreline looking for a place to have dinner.

Since almost every place was accessible from the beach, we rarely used the jeep we rented. We stayed in a couple of new beach hotels on our list to try, deeming them acceptable, but not particularly unique in any way.

After a few days, we wanted to explore beyond the familiar, so we went looking for a new place to stay. As we wandered south along the shore, we spotted a small hand-lettered "en renta" sign perched on an isolated stretch of beach. Exploring further, we came upon a one-bedroom casita and began looking to find someone to ask if it was available. In the distance, we could see a young Mexican man in a wide-brimmed straw hat, and we waved to him, indicating we wanted to rent the place. Through hand-signals and broken Spanish, we learned that it was free until Saturday, so we could stay until then. This little place was different for us. It was totally quiet and unpretentious…perfect for a spiritual holiday. We hardly saw another person during our stay. We had a couple of days of peaceful introspection, and then it was time to go.

The next morning, we hopped in the Jeep and drove forty kilometers south to Punta Allen, a sleepy fishing village at the very end of the only road that extends along the beach from Tulum. It takes you through the "Sian Kan" biosphere, a nature preserve that looks just like Tulum without benefit of gentrification.

The drive took us all day. This was partly due to the primitive road conditions, but mostly because we took our time and stopped frequently. Slowing down to stroll a stretch of virgin shoreline gave us a feeling of harmony with nature. After taking numerous photos and watching pelicans, as they soared and dipped head first into the sea, we looked for somewhere to eat lunch. When we stopped at a funky little beach bar along the way, we saw that they had casitas for rent. Tempted by the complete isolation and immersion in the wild, we asked if we could stay the night. Surprise! All three casitas were booked, so we continued on our journey, only to return to Tulum by evening.

Considering where to go next, I recalled a hotel we had seen on one of our walks the previous week. The architecture was interesting, and I had seen various groups of yoga-esque people wandering the premises, chatting quietly on orange beach chairs. Someone was sitting alone facing the sea, lost in peaceful meditation on a fallen driftwood branch. By then, Curtis and I had had enough "alone time" and both felt ready for some company.

As we entered the aptly named Casa Magna, we were immediately impressed by the sheer scale of the thirty-foot ceilings, massive expanses of tile and stone, all contributing to the haunting beauty of this unusual place. Primitive wood finishes, whimsical details, artisanal furniture and a deliberate lack of polish were all part of the charm, defining what we came to know as the *eco-chic* trend that had swept through this part of Mexico. It turned out that this hotel was the remodeled former villa of Colombian drug lord Pablo Escobar, abandoned after his death in 1993. Casa Magna had the simplicity we wanted, but retained a trace of stylishness, and this appealed to us, even though we shied away from other large accommodations in the area. The enormity of the villa belied its uber-hip, spiritually-attuned culture, complete with trippy music, dim lighting and a laidback staff.

This particular week, Casa Magna was inhabited by a group from California on a yoga retreat. The evening meals were served family style, so we shared tables out on the terrace with the participants. Curious about the set up, I peeked into the yoga studio. The room was breathtaking—absurdly high ceilings, yoga mats arranged on the limestone floor, so elegant and simple, with enormous windows open to a beautiful vista of the sea. I was smitten. The whole villa had the atmosphere of a monastery, and we basked in the quiet that night as we drifted off to sleep, the sound of the rolling surf in the distance. Even in this spectacular setting I was able to reconnect with my original intention to keep it simple. As a new me began to emerge, I felt the importance of my prior status fade into history.

As stylish as Casa Magna appeared, the lack of modern convenience was a constant reminder of how far off the beaten track we were. In the early years when we first visited Tulum, the only way to reach the expanse of hotels along the shore was by a primitive dirt road comprised of huge potholes and stretches of sandy rubble. Most hotels had electricity for just a few hours a day, and no one had internet or phone service. Now, the road is paved, hotels offer fashionably rustic accommodations and restaurants boast sophisticated menus with New York prices. These days, everyone has a cell phone and internet connection, though the reception is still delightfully (but sometimes frustratingly) unpredictable.

I experienced this frustration one day when I checked my voice mail and realized that the CEO of Liz Claiborne had been trying to reach me for days. Once I was able to access the hotel wireless, my laptop showed emails from his assistant as well. In minutes, I could feel the tension begin to permeate the peaceful aura I'd been cultivating all week. Even the voicemail message—"Please advise your correct mailing address, because I have something to send to you, and it seems we have more than one on file"—annoyed me.

It was so typical of the corporate dysfunction that the HR department, with whom I had been corresponding for months, could not provide the executive floor with my correct mailing address. After all, they had been sending multiple documents to me, not to mention my paycheck. In no time, I snapped right back to the high-strung fashionista I thought I'd left behind.

Of course, I felt compelled to respond immediately. It had always been my practice to return calls or emails promptly, and that habit was still deeply ingrained. There was no cell phone signal on the beach where we were that day, so I threw a *pareo* over my bikini, and hopped into the Jeep and journeyed up the road towards town and cell phone service. Nervous as I was, inside I knew it was ridiculous how I was willingly racing towards mayhem. Checking my phone every few seconds, it was a matter of minutes before I found a spot to park, where my phone showed a few bars of signal. I dialed the number, my stomach in a knot.

I reached his assistant and I was surprised when he was immediately available for my call. His cheerful tone was even more surprising.

"I am so happy to talk to you, Sigrid. We have been trying to reach you! I have a proposal I think you will find very exciting. We want to relaunch the SIGRID OLSEN brand."

I thought: Wait. What? Didn't you just close it down? Now you want to resurrect it? I listened, unable to speak. "O-kaaay...," I finally uttered as a signal for him to elaborate.

"Yes, we think we have a fantastic opportunity to bring back the brand but in an unconventional new way. We have the opportunity to offer SIGRID OLSEN exclusively through the TV channel. We figure we can do 100 million in about 3 years. But, of course, we need you to help us with this."

I felt my heart constrict. "Go on," I said.

"Sigrid, you have a following, and we feel we can re-appoint the consumer by offering the most iconic product classifications from the past. We will go through the archives and select the best sellers and recreate them for sale on television. They will handle all the sourcing and production, sales and distribution, so it's an easy transition for us to be back in business. It would be a healthy business with fewer sizes, no worry about returns, and built-in marketing. I'd like you to think about all the product classifications we can sell, starting with sweaters, but expanding to all lifestyle categories in the future."

I said, "With all due respect, I think you may be underestimating the complexity of the design process. It took a very experienced and talented team of designers to come up with the level of detail, the unique color palettes and all the special touches that made our garments bestsellers. The factories had to learn our methods and we worked hard to ensure the quality of the garments was top notch, especially the sweaters."

I worried this new venue would never be able to do the brand justice. I also worried what working with not one, but two mega-corporations would do to my still fragile peace of mind. But what he said next roused my dormant ego and caused me to consider the possibility of being a designer in demand again.

"That's what we need you for."

Aha! I thought. "I *do* like being *needed*." A sleepy little spark of self-importance started to awaken inside me and I felt myself respond to the familiar thrill of being valued. Even though I thought I had come to terms with my new, simplified lifestyle and serene self-image. Even though I *knew better*.

I thanked him and asked for time to think about it, agreeing to contact him when I was back home in a week or so. The whole conversation left me in turmoil, and I needed time to process it all. I promised to email his assistant with my proper contact information and said goodbye.

"Damn!" I thought. "I have been doing so well letting go of nagging thoughts and now I have to make a decision. My equanimity took a back seat, while I replayed the conversation in my head.

My brain was buzzing as I bounced down the road in the Jeep towards the beach hotel where Curtis was waiting for me, no doubt curious about the subject of the phone call. When I parked and approached the beach, I felt relieved as usual to be embraced by the uplifting expanse of sea and sky on the horizon. In a daze, I crossed the sand to join Curtis under the *palapa* where he was reading a book.

"So?"

I recounted for him the details of the conversation. I was clearly ruffled by the emotional conflict the business proposal had sparked. We discussed all our options, fantasized about the influx of money it would provide, and weighed the pros and cons. I could feel the clash between my internal forces: adrenaline pumping from the excitement of it all and my heart beating madly to reach my brain with the message: "Don't do it." In any given minute I would seesaw between the outrageous appeal of this exceptional opportunity and the anguish of abandoning the path of self-discovery I was on.

I decided to sleep on it. Why make a decision before I needed to? I would just go on with my vacation and see where my intuition led me. I passed the rest of the day in an altered state. I was grumpy and short with Curtis. I was hot and sweaty and everything irritated me. I hardly recognized myself. It had been weeks since I'd felt this kind of stress and expressed any sort of complaint. Hmmm…maybe my intuition was having an unspoken conversation with me. I didn't like how I felt, and I certainly didn't approve of my behavior.

I tried to examine it from every angle. The words "hierarchy of values" echoed in my mind. This was the first real test of my willpower. Was I willing to sacrifice autonomy to be part of a big machine again so soon?

I didn't believe, after everything I had been through, that the corporations' infatuation with me would last past the first few seasons. I also knew what an enormous undertaking it would be to coordinate all the agendas—both corporations and mine. Especially mine. My goal to keep my sanity, for one. I had expended enough energy fighting city hall without success. I wasn't sure I had it in me to do it again. I knew my dedication to the purity of design, standards of quality and faithful execution of artistic details was a tall order, especially in this scenario. I admit the idea of being in the public eye again was seductive, and I suspected I would do well on camera, though it was a completely new venue for me.

Of course, even then, I was keenly aware of the huge volume (translation: big money) that such a deal could garner, since I had been wooed many times in the past. Then I thought about what it would feel like losing control of my brand once again. The memory of my personal heartache these last few years was still a fresh wound. I remembered feeling helpless as the soul of my company was deconstructed bit by bit and replaced with a hollow replica, all in the name of profit and progress. I was sure I didn't want to live through that again. I also felt instinctively there was something very important I needed to do first.

By that evening I knew I had made my decision. I waited until I returned home to officially decline. I knew it would be a difficult phone call and it was. When we spoke, it was very brief. I was nervous, not knowing what kind of reaction my refusal would trigger under the circumstances. It did not come naturally for me to say no. I braced myself and thanked him for thinking of me, stating simply, while I appreciated the opportunity, whatever new enterprise I would choose next would have to be my own. He was gracious and accepted my decision without any argument. It was done.

The choice made, I silently congratulated myself for protecting my hard-won independence and for giving my evolving inner artist a voice. Meanwhile, my "compulsively creative" side was still alive and well. As relaxed as I had become, I still felt the tug of wanting to *do* something more. I wanted to break new ground.

I let go of all of my preconceptions about business and my position in it and opened to inventing myself anew. The clues to this undiscovered territory were right there on the beach in Tulum. It just took me a while to realize it.

The next day at Casa Magna, I joined Curtis for breakfast after morning yoga. He was engaged in conversation with two women who were there on retreat. When he introduced me by name, I realized they were excited to meet "the" Sigrid Olsen. I was flattered, humbled and, frankly, surprised. It's a sensation I have gotten used to.

Since that day, I have been repeatedly amazed by the recognition my name receives all over the country. When I was working I never knew how far the brand reached because, as a fashion executive, I didn't often encounter real customers, except at well-publicized events. Now, on the beach in Mexico, I was face-to-face with two of them. We chatted for a while—about fashion, about yoga, about our affection for Tulum. They both expressed sadness about the demise of my line, while I made my usual sympathetic comments and tried to turn the conversation towards the positive. It wasn't the first time I would do this, and certainly far from the last.

This chance meeting was the first clue that Tulum would figure prominently in my future and spurred my creative mind in a new direction. It got me thinking about how I could harness the name recognition and good will that my fashion brand prompted in people.

I realized there was something about this connection with other women, especially spiritual seekers, that appealed to me. It touched on the desire I had throughout my career to make my business more meaningful.

I wasn't able to pinpoint just what I could actually do to satisfy that urge. I knew it had to do with inspiring and being inspired. It was Curtis who first suggested an idea that would incorporate my artistic talent, my love of yoga, and my desire to re-ignite my connection with all the women who remembered me as a designer.

Observing the unique attraction of yoga retreats in this particular locale, he proposed:

"Why don't you offer a retreat to all your customers? They would be thrilled to spend a vacation with Sigrid Olsen in Mexico! Why not give them the uplifting experience you did with your stores, but just without selling clothes?"

I was slightly taken aback, stating the obvious: "But, I don't teach yoga."

Before actually embracing a new idea, I have a habit of always bringing up reasons why I can't do it. Eventually, I saw that the discovery I had made on this very beach was something I could share. It came to me as if in bold italics:

The more I quieted my mind and found balance through yoga and meditation, the more creative I felt.

I had come to Tulum for a transformative experience, and I knew there were many more women out there in transition, especially during this era of layoffs and economic upheaval. I realized that there was *value* in taking time to reconnect with myself, and I was sure I wasn't alone in needing this.

I observed myself under these new circumstances. Without the external pressure of producing beauty under a deadline, I was free to explore and perhaps rediscover my purest, most creative self. Aware that creativity is defined differently for each of us, I concluded that the one factor that humans have in common is that we all love to create—to have an idea and then see it come to fruition.

I see the unrestrained delight small children take in making things and I wondered—what happens to us as adults that we become self-conscious and lose the joy of creating just for fun?

One gift my parents imparted to me was endless encouragement to do what I love and not be shy about it. Others are not so lucky. My artistic inclination and confident spontaneity were assets I could use to help those who wanted to unleash dormant creativity but hadn't the faintest idea how to do it.

Our Mexican escape taught me how to approach this revelatory process with a few simple practices: simplify your surroundings, release your attachment to "stuff", live close to nature and release stress through yoga. The retreat idea became an opportunity to incorporate everything I had learned. I decided to call my new enterprise "Inspiration Retreats', thereby solidifying the real purpose of the concept—to inspire and be inspired.

I pulled out my sketchbook and began to plan, noting both the practical considerations (where and when will we hold it and how much will it cost?) with the ideological content, (what wisdom will I share? how can I best inspire? will people really come?) If they do, I want them to be blown away. Even though I was here to relax, I could feel my Type A persona spring into action. But this time, it felt good to apply my skills to something so close to my heart.

I called my sister Martha, at home in Martha's Vineyard, and shared my idea with her, hoping she might agree to be the yoga instructor for the retreat. She had spent several years in residence at Kripalu, the yoga center in Lenox, Massachusetts, studying movement therapy and leading yoga teacher trainings. She traveled to Peru to study shamanism and now added "shamanic healing" to her resume. Clearly, she knew a lot more about these things than I did. All the years I was globe-trotting and stressing out, I envied the alternate path she had taken and now I was about to embark on a similar journey. By the time I hung up the phone, she was enthusiastically on board and I was elated.

Before we checked out of Casa Magna, we informed the manager we wanted to reserve the property for a retreat in January of 2009. "Quite the planner! A year in advance!" I'm sure she was thinking that as we gave her the dates. She seemed preoccupied with the retreat in residence, but we left satisfied that we had set the scene for the future event, and we were excited.

As it turned out, crazy circumstances prevented us from hosting our retreat at Casa Magna in 2009. Months after we left Mexico, I was talking with some friends who own property in Tulum, and I chattered on excitedly about the retreat we were planning at Casa Magna for next winter, when they said, "I thought that place had closed. Didn't you hear what happened there last May?"

I said, "No. You must be thinking of some other place. We haven't heard anything about the hotel closing or our retreat dates being cancelled!"

Right away I Googled "Casa Magna Tulum" and learned the truth.

Headline: "Casa Magna Resort in Tulum Seized by Mexican Mafia."

Great. Mexico makes people nervous enough, but this was a real setback! Here's an excerpt from the article in the *New York Post*:

> *"Imagine booking a much-needed vacation to*
> *Tulum at the Casa Magna eco-resort, a favorite*
> *retreat for celebs like Drew Barrymore, and*

arriving at the hotel only to find that the "Mexican Mafia" has seized the place with armed men and helicopters on the beach, prompting the staff and the owner to flee. Exactly who pulled off the raid remains unclear. But one art collector received an e-mail recently from the hotel stating, "We have run into some unexpected problems with the Mexican government involving a land dispute that has affected Casa Magna's stability. The people we lease from are being sued and the opposing party has appeared out of the woodwork with papers giving them temporary occupation."

This was followed by irate *Trip Advisor* posts online by guests who had been in residence there for a wedding and were evacuated mid-stay. It dawned on me quickly—if I wanted to go through with my plans for a retreat in Tulum, I had to find an alternative. We ended up renting our friend's villa and booking all the guest rooms at Coqui Coqui, a beautiful old stone hotel and spa next door. We lost some participants in the transition, especially after the Casa Magna news, but eventually, we gathered a small but remarkable group of women to join us, and the retreat was on, almost exactly one year after the idea was born.

I knew the first retreat would be special, a prototype for the future, so I made sure I spared no expense and left everyone with the sense they'd gotten far more than they bargained for. It was worth every penny. I noted, even as I saw the red ink, that there was a nugget of gold in this idea. The satisfaction I got from seeing it all come together provided a pivotal role in the re-design of my life.

We were a mixed congregation of women: doctor, lawyer, health care manager, buyer, spa director and business executive. In no time, the titles faded away, leaving only the faintest imprint of our former selves as the bonding progressed. We became a group of kindred spirits on an adventure of self-discovery. I thought to myself the day everyone showed up, "What a diverse and interesting group". Comparing our collection of guests to ingredients in a soup, the flavor subtly changed with each woman who arrived on the scene lending her particular seasoning to the mélange brewing in the pot. By the time everyone made it there, we were a tasty stew for sure.

I wasn't sure how my daily agenda would hold up, but I was pleasantly surprised when I saw that my careful planning, balanced by my easy-going flexibility and fortified by Martha's capable guidance, laid the groundwork for what looked to be a productive and life-changing week for everyone. Each morning, we would gather as a group to greet the day, with Martha leading us through a few simple yoga poses and breathing exercises. The rising sun illuminated our faces as we stretched and bowed toward the glittering surface of the sea. That alone softened any rough edges that remained. Who could resist the overpowering beauty of this place?

After breakfast, I set the table with paint and paper where the plates and forks had just been and the art workshops took shape. A few were afraid of what to expect since they didn't consider themselves artistic, but their anxiety was hushed the moment I announced that the first day they would only be allowed to paint stripes. That took the pressure off right away.

I find that taking it down to this very basic exercise is a great equalizer. Everyone can relax and enjoy the feel of the brush on the paper, the blending of color and the freedom to play without worrying about the outcome.

If that isn't freeing enough, the next step is to take the pages of painted stripes and cut them up, in essence recycling them for another use in collage. By then most people let go of any devotion they may have felt for their paintings, a tangible lesson in detachment.

The art sessions that followed in the next few days were similar to this, each one adding a new element, including life-affirming words we conjured up during a guided meditation and pasted onto our final "Life Vision" collage on the last day. We also collected a batch of negative words in an effort to let go of their hold on us, and then we burned them in a ceremonial bonfire. The retreat progressed like a dream sequence of yoga poses and shamanic visions, complete with a moonlit rooftop gathering and constant animated chatter as a soundtrack. Laughter permeated all our gatherings.

My retreat structure has evolved significantly since this first one, but the essence remains the same: escape from the stress of daily life, join with other like-minded spirits, relax in a beautiful place, replenish body and soul and re-connect with your innermost self. It was and is a transformative experience, not just for my guests, but for me as well.

That first winter after my career about-face, we went to Tulum three times. I was drawn to the healing power, wildness and simplicity of the place. Being there erased the barriers between myself and nature, making me feel grounded and alive in a way that being at home in my comfortable house did not.

I continued to practice yoga, feeling my heart open more each time I stretched, hands to the sky in my favorite sequence—Surya Namaskar—Salutation to the Sun. I liked being around people doing the same things. It made me feel less alone and reminded me what I love most about yoga—-regardless of age, status, income level, shape or color, we are all essentially the same—human beings, flawed but hopeful, busy but mindful, afraid but willing to try.

My Tulum Escape provided a window to a new world for me. I got to look at things from another vantage point and began to sense that there was indeed an alternate path I could follow into my future. It was the first step in my awakening.

~ 232 ~

Tears in My Ears

"Loss and joy sit side by side in my heart. They coexist."
—Sigrid Olsen

This book is about my journey and, as you can see, it hasn't necessarily followed a predictable path. Tulum was only the beginning. There, I recaptured my heart's desire. I promised myself to make happiness and fulfillment the core concepts of my life's ambition. I was ready to take a spiritual leap. But another lesson came when I was faced, once again, with an unexpected overwhelming obstacle.

I was just recovering from my second major upheaval, first breast cancer and then the loss of my business, when another personal storm blew into my life like a hurricane. Like before, tragedy presented another powerful lesson of impermanence. Here is what I learned: just when everything seems perfect, life can shake every bit of hard-won serenity from one's limbs like a gale force wind. It wonderful to fall in love with every moment, but it's wise not to get too attached. Embracing change is a tricky business. These days, when I'm really happy, I have a little voice inside that says:

"Don't get too attached to this. It's fleeting."

More than just a warning, it calls for a shift of perspective, which allows me to hold the extraordinary moment a little more gently. I loosen my grip, giving it some wiggle room, like a plant that needs loose soil for the roots to expand. The secret is to keep the beauty of the moment in your heart, yet give it the freedom to fly away, knowing it will return again someday.

Instead of grasping, I try to believe that there's always more where that came from. Another sunset. Another glimpse of the divine.

So what happens when peace so carefully cultivated is suddenly shattered? All the beauty doesn't just disappear. In fact, my losses have helped me understand a most important lesson: our time here is short and each moment is precious. Life is an uncertain alchemy—a mysterious mixture of emotions that make us *human*.

It does us no good to insist on happiness all the time. Despair and joy can sit side by side in our heart, and this is perfectly natural. Neither is permanent. There is nothing like losing a loved one abruptly, without warning, that teaches this lesson so profoundly. I came face-to-face with this one sunny morning in Sarasota when, out of nowhere, Curtis had a heart attack and was gone. Just like that.

Like a snapshot in living color, the day my husband died stands out vividly in my memory. I was having one of those "I am in love with life" moments on a blue-sky, Sunday morning in our sun-filled apartment overlooking Sarasota Bay. Feeling this happy triggered the subliminal voice inside my head:

"Don't get too attached", it whispered, as I typed the final few words of a blog I was writing.

Just as I wrote "Life is full of surprises. I wonder what's next?" and hit the *submit* button, there was a strident knock on my door. I was alone in the apartment, waiting for Curtis to return from a long bike ride on Longboat Key. He'd been gone for over two hours, which seemed odd, but if he had taken the long road all the way to Anna Maria Island, sometimes it took that long, so I wasn't concerned. The knocking was loud and insistent. I rose from my seat, mildly annoyed because no one we knew ever knocked, and I wasn't expecting any visitors. When I opened the door, a uniformed policeman was standing there with a look of concern on his face. I was puzzled.

"Are you Curtis Sanders' wife?" He asked quietly.

"Yes. What can I do for you?"

"Well, ma'am, your husband was riding his bicycle out on Longboat Key and must have had some sort of episode. He was picked up by the EMT's and transported to Sarasota Memorial. They want you to come and meet them there."

I was taken aback, but only slightly worried. He'd been having some dizzy spells lately and it was pretty hot in the mid-March Florida sun. "Is he OK?" I asked, my concern elevating when the officer couldn't provide a straight answer.

"I don't know, ma'am. They just asked me to come and let you know."

"Of course. Let me just get my things and I will head right over. Thank you."

I still remember what I was wearing as I dashed out to the hospital (J. Crew grey v-neck tee shirt and my favorite orange cotton cropped jeans) not because I have an uncanny retention of fashion details, but because I wore the same outfit for the next three days, unable to pull together anything else.

It was a short ten-minute drive that I managed by pure automatic pilot. Pulling in to the emergency room entrance, I left the car with the valet and rushed to the front desk, mentioning that my husband had been brought in by the paramedics. They directed me to the ER and I stopped again at the desk there and gave his name. I was politely asked to take a seat in the waiting area and a doctor would be right with me. *Not good.*

I fidgeted as I waited what seemed like hours but was probably more like ten minutes. Eventually, the doctor came in and explained, "Your husband was seen lying next to his bike by some passersby, and they called 911. He suffered some sort of seizure or heart attack and was resuscitated successfully in the ambulance."

"Phew," I thought, with a soft exhale. I hadn't realized I was holding my breath.

"Then the EMT's brought him here, where his heart failed again, but this time, we were unsuccessful. I am so sorry, but we lost him."

Wait. What? I felt my mouth go dry and my whole body started to vibrate. This was impossible. He was fine just a few hours ago. I couldn't comprehend the idea that this was it. Utterly final. I could not absorb this bizarre reality that was being served up.

"Holy Shit" is what I said. Part of me felt apologetic to have cursed in public, but it was utterly warranted. The news was so all encompassing, so absurdly irrevocable, there really was not much left to say. I sat stunned in the harsh light of the hospital waiting room, following my thoughts through multiple crazy corridors, trying to imagine what life would be like after this moment. Each thought was like a dead end street, leading nowhere. I could barely grasp what had happened, much less see beyond the next few minutes.

They asked me if I wanted to see him and, reluctantly, I went into the adjacent room where he lay in his biking clothes. But he wasn't there. It was absolutely clear to me that whatever life force that constituted the man I knew and loved was long gone, and an empty replica was in his place.

I wanted to be with his spirit in the sky, but not with his body in this metallic hospital room.

It didn't take long, however, for hospital procedure to kick into action, and they brought in a social worker to help me sort through the next steps. They did it with compassion, but it was too much, too soon. I was ill-equipped to make any major decisions. I picked the first funeral home on the list they gave me. All I remember is that it began with the letter "A" and when they called the number it was out of service. *Perfect.* I don't remember a thing after that. But within an hour it was wrapped up, and I was free to go.

Did I need anything? They asked me, gently. It took me a while to respond. The sound landed on my ears, but the words took time to make sense.

"Thank you. I don't think so."

There was a long pause.

"Oh, yes. One thing. Can you please bring my ticket out to the valet?" My hands were shaking as I scrambled in my purse to locate it. I knew one thing for sure. I couldn't tolerate even one minute standing on the sidewalk in front of the ER, waiting for my car. "That would really help. Thanks so much."

One of the many things I loved about our new life in Florida was the apartment building where we lived. The facade is bright pink and resembles a wedding cake, with expansive sunset views from every unit. Some of the residents nicknamed it the Pink Poodle. Its small size enabled us to know almost everyone and, for a while, it felt like we had adopted a new family.

When I arrived there, after my trance-like drive home, a group of my neighbors were having an impromptu meeting just inside the lobby. As usual, on my arrival, I was greeted with friendly hellos.

"Hey, Sigrid. Nice to see you!" And then the customary, "How are you?" It was an innocent question.

I wasn't sure how to answer. I couldn't just say fine and then head upstairs. How does one communicate such a monumental shift in one's entire existence? I was in uncharted territory. So I answered honestly.

"Not so good. I just came from the hospital. Curtis had a heart attack while he was out riding his bike and…" Major pause. "He passed away." I felt myself go numb.

It was as though a thick blanket of fog descended on all of us. They all stared at me in disbelief, and once the truth sunk in, they enveloped me in one huge hug with choruses of "Oh no! I'm so sorry. I can't believe this. Are you OK? What can we do?"

It was only then that the tears came. My eyes welled-up and I felt like I was liquefied by their kindness. My heart finally broke open and, for the first time, I felt the depth of what had happened.

After a brief exchange I excused myself and somehow navigated upstairs to my perch on the fourth floor. I needed a moment.

The sea was sparkling on the bay below me as I sat dazed on my balcony. "The sun is still shining. That's good," I thought. It was just like me to find something positive. As if magnetized, I was drawn to the outdoors. I let the midday heat penetrate my frozen soul in hopes I might find comfort there. I saw his face in the sky, imagining the ethereal Curtis drifting up into the heavens. It is the oddest sensation to have someone there one moment and then permanently gone the next.

Unsure of how long I had been sitting there, eventually I realized I needed to let people close to me know what had happened. That was a pretty long list—my kids, my sister, Lisa, Curtis' kids, my Dad, his best friends in California. I started with my kids. Erik was the first one to answer.

I blurted out the news, and he was shocked and so sweet. "God, Mom, are you OK? That's awful. What can we do for you?"

Writing this, I see a pattern that was repeated time after time. It's the natural reaction sequence—shock, concern, empathy, outpouring of love, offer to help. It happened the same way with every phone conversation. The calls to my step-kids were the hardest. How do you tell someone, two to three-thousand miles away that his or her father is gone forever? In a flash, any chance to see him again is extinguished. They were heartbroken, and it deepened my suffering to hear the pain in their voices. I could only share their anguish and tell them I loved them.

Not knowing I was in shock, I proceeded to take care of business. I talked to the coroner, the organ donor people and the funeral home. I cancelled appointments and dinners on our schedules. When I got my sister Lisa on the phone, she asked if I needed her to come. That hadn't occurred to me. I felt okay—stunned, but still functional. I didn't see any reason to disrupt her life.

"No, I'm alright. There's nothing really to do. But thanks."

Long pause.

"Are you sure?"

I took a deep breath. I felt my throat constrict and tears moisten my eyes. In a small voice that somehow prevailed over my denial, I said, "Yes. Please come."

She was there the next day. Erik and Brita followed soon after, and it felt like some sort of heavenly gift to have all the people I loved around me with no real agenda, just uninterrupted time to simply *be* together. We hadn't had that in years.

News spread quickly, and friends were calling, coming by and dropping off lovely bags of groceries from Whole Foods, knowing that pies and casseroles aren't really my thing. The offerings I appreciated most were those I didn't ask for. My neighbor brought me a beautiful green salad even after I said I wasn't hungry. I devoured it gratefully. A dear friend from Massachusetts was on vacation with her family in Boca Raton, and without asking, she drove the three and a half hours west to see me and spent the night. I will never forget that act of selfless caring.

I learned quickly that, in this fugue state of grief, I couldn't make any decisions, especially ones about what I needed. It was much better when people simply brought or did things without asking. That kind of unspoken thoughtfulness and generosity kept me from falling apart.

The other thing that helped me hold it together was yoga. It didn't take long before I was back at it, needing the quietude, the introspection and, especially, the support of this informal family to help me heal. The studio that Curtis and I went to most regularly (and I still do) is located not far from downtown Sarasota. A collection of small wooden bungalows around an overgrown central courtyard, in a slightly sketchy part of town, it feels like a cozy throwback to my hippie days. Whenever I walk up the path to the studio, yoga mat tucked under my arm, I feel like I'm coming home.

We had three favorite instructors there, and they knew us well. By the time I got to class about a week after his death, my teacher was aware and ready to give me the big, beautiful hug I needed. As I rolled out my mat, I started to feel myself relax. Soft music played, and the sun filtered softly through the matchstick blinds onto the golden wood floor. I needed this.

Arranging myself into a seated half lotus, I settled in for a brief meditation before class started. Deep breath, and then another. In the profound silence, I began to feel an intense wave of grief wash over me. I started to quietly weep at the exceptional purity of the moment. There were no distractions to temper my emotions—the sensation of sadness was neither good nor bad. It just *was*. It actually felt wonderful to allow my heart to break open like this.

Once I began the more rigorous work of flowing through the poses, the tears paused, while I set my whole being into motion. For over an hour, I worked through kinks that had knotted my limbs and gripped my lower back from the stress of the last several days. It felt good to be empowered in some way. My body responded with gratitude.

As usual, I finished up my practice with a headstand and then slowly made my way into *savasana*, the final resting pose. Lying prone on my mat, imagining my muscles melting into the benevolent support of the wood floor under me, the warm wash of heartache returned. Overcome by emotion, I began to cry silently, without holding back, and the wetness dripped down both sides of my face. "I have tears in my ears", I thought, simultaneously amused by the cleverness of my rhyme and awed by the primal power of the emotion. All I could do was passively let them flow. This release is what I came for and it touched the very heart of me.

We ended the session in a seated position with a shared chant of *Om*. Positioned directly in front of our instructor, I opened my eyes after the final bow of *Namaste* to see her staring straight at me with a compassionate look of recognition on her lovely face. No other words were necessary. *Namaste*. It simply means *the divine light in me honors the divine light in you*. An unspoken recognition of what it is to be two humans connecting on this earth. That simple, yet monumental, gesture was enough to refill my empty heart. It was comforting to know that this unconditional acceptance and love was there for me whenever I needed it. I needed it quite often and I went to class several times a week to refill my depleted reserves.

The grieving process doesn't have a predictable timeline—beginning, middle, end. It's cruel and mercurial. Sometimes it seems to have disappeared and life goes on as usual, with laughter and music and glasses of wine with dinner. Then suddenly there's a sneak attack at three a.m. and you are left panting in the dark, or manically pacing the floor in the moonlight. That's when you realize that you are really alone. The whole world is sleeping, and you are left to wrestle solo with unruly thoughts.

I felt *untethered*. There was no word that captured my current state as well. By definition, it means free, released. But it also means without an anchor. The conflicting significance rang so true. Suddenly there were no boundaries—I could do anything I wanted, any time I wanted. There was no husband, no children, and no restrictions on my life. But I also felt like a balloon that wasn't tied to anything, ascending into the atmosphere, in danger of vanishing into the ether.

Finding the courage to reach out and ask for help did not come easily to me. I discovered though, by just speaking my truth, everyone was more than willing to show up. Most of the time, showing up was all that was needed.

I busied myself planning how to commemorate him properly, determined to include all the people important to us. I decided that we would need three separate memorial services. Because of our peripatetic lifestyle, we had cherished people scattered around the country, all of whom would want to celebrate his life. Trying to limit it to one location would be impossible.

The first gathering took place at the *Pink Poodle*. It was scheduled for sunset, because the light on our west-facing shoreline was extraordinary, bordering on supernatural. Instead of the rapturous display of color we expected, a dense white fog rolled in just as our collection of friends and neighbors arrived. It was never foggy like this in the evening, especially in April. It felt more like San Francisco than Sarasota, which was eerie, since that was where Curtis lived when we met…and Northern California was his happy place. His presence was tangible in the cool mist of the evening as we sat remembering him with anecdotes, slide shows and a potluck banquet orchestrated by friends.

About a week later, Erik, Brita and I flew out to the West Coast to celebrate him with his family in Marin County. It was a bit of a challenge to coordinate the memorial service long-distance, but I managed with the help of my step-kids Chris, Dusty and Katie, and Curtis's best friends, who hosted the reception afterwards. There is a beautiful spot on a lake not far from where he used to live in

Novato, a flat green meadow with majestic willow trees presiding over the still water under a brilliant sun. Lots of people spoke; it was joyful and heartbreaking at the same time. The highlight of the day came when, unexpectedly, Tyler and Jake, Curtis's young grandsons stood at the podium to speak, each taking turns at the mic with brave little voices. They were so small, they had to stand on a milk crate to reach the microphone. The audience was rapt with attention.

Jake: "This is a very sad day for us."

Tyler: "Nobody knew he was going to die so soon. He just wanted to ride his bike." He sighed, glanced at Jake, took a deep breath, and continued. "He always said when it is your time to go, it is your time to go. We will all miss him a lot." Long pause. "It won't be the same without him."

Then they both hopped down, and there was an electrified hush across the audience. Their impromptu speech slayed every one of us. The feeling of togetherness that this kind of shared moment creates is a gift that so often goes unnoticed. Usually, we are focused on the loss, not the gain. We were all in pain, but the air was infused with love. The climax of the evening was when a dramatic rainbow appeared above the trees outside the house, just as dinner was served. Those closest to Curtis knew that *Over the Rainbow* was his favorite song, and he frequently reminded us, with a smile, that he wanted it played at his funeral. That night, we gathered on the deck, arm-in-arm, faces turned up to the darkening sky, certain he was there among us.

The next day, the whole combined family drove over the mountains to Dillon Beach, on the northern coast of Marin County, just south of Bodega Bay. There were seventeen of us. All the grandchildren were there, even Dillon Curtis, who was as yet unborn. Named after this beach and his grandfather, his name holds profound significance…it's a shame he and Curtis never met.

The seacoast was characteristically blustery and cool, even though it was spring in California. Under a sky heavy with clouds, Dusty and Chris perched on a rocky promontory to disperse the ashes into the surf that pounded below. Something about the turbulent Pacific Ocean, the sunless sky and the fierce beauty of this unspoiled place felt sacred to all of us, and it sealed a permanent bond that has endured long after the memory of that day.

The third memorial service was the most well attended. Nearly a hundred friends, old and new, gathered at the Cultural Center on Rocky Neck in Gloucester, which is a beautiful, repurposed Christian Science Church with lovely light filtering through arched windows and a cozy small-town feel. I can't even remember who was there, because it's is a blur—a dreamy montage of sweet faces and kind words, with our dear friend, Jamie's acapella version of *I'll be Seeing You*, as the soundtrack finale. My heart felt empty and overflowing at the same time. I remember resting a grateful head on my son Erik's shoulder, overcome with emotion, listening to one after another of our friends share heartwarming stories and anecdotes about Curtis with the crowd.

As a mother, there is something so touching when the tables turn, and your kids are there for you after so many years of being their caregiver. Learning to receive love and accept help was the remarkable lesson I learned from all this sorrow.

In May, two months after Curtis passed, I returned to Gloucester for the summer, just as we had done every summer since we moved part-time to Sarasota. Adjusting to the transition between two residences was always difficult, but this year it was excruciating. Loneliness (or rather, the anticipation of loneliness) gripped me. However, the advantage of living in a community like Rocky Neck is the sense of inclusiveness it provides. Anytime the solitude was unbearable, the chatter in my brain too loud, I could simply walk out my door and, inevitably, I would run into someone I knew and engage in conversation, maybe even catch an impromptu meal and glass of wine at a local restaurant.

Thankfully, I had lots of company that summer. My friend Lucia (yes, she has the same name as my mother, but pronounces it *Lucy*) stayed with me the majority of the season, happy to escape the city. It's valuable to have a friend who melds with whatever unfolds. She somehow harmonized quite happily with frequent extended visits from my two grandchildren, who were ten and seven at the time. The four of us cohabited in the small one-bedroom house, and she helped me operate my gallery. People were coming and going constantly. I couldn't have done it that summer without her. She helped me reimagine my space and rearrange furniture to adjust to my now single occupancy, with a sensitivity that bespoke her lifelong vocation as a trauma nurse, accented by a flair for fashion and decorating.

By October, it was time to head south again. This time, my sister Lisa was my copilot. She agreed to accompany me on the long drive in my two-seater Audi TT and offered to stay as long as I needed. The fact that she would enjoy the warmth of a Florida winter assuaged my guilt for taking her away from her life, her husband and her role as caregiver for our aging father. She ended up staying until April. It was soothing to have her there—someone who was okay with silence, easy to live with, totally supportive and there only when I needed her.

The people in my life—my family, my neighbors, friends both north and south—they became my touchstones. I created a Facebook group called *Circle of Friends*, and it gave me a safe place to air my rawest emotions and find solace in their responses.

It was like reaching out into the darkness and finding multiple tiny points of light.

The Eight Things

1 CONNECT TO NATURE
Take a walk on the beach.
Stare up at the sky.
Gather wildflowers.
Howl at the moon.

2 INHABIT YOUR BODY
Breathe. Move. Dance.
Make love.
Do anything that makes you
feel awake and alive.

3 FIND A COMMUNITY
Seek out people who are
honest and fun,
who will listen
and tell the truth.

4 SIMPLIFY
Literally and metaphorically,
clear out the clutter that
complicates your life.

5 QUIET DOWN
Turn off the noise.
Enjoy some solitude.
Tune inward.
Surrender to the silence.

6 OPEN YOUR HEART
Be generous with your
time and talent.
Giving always
comes back to you.

7 CREATE
Make something.
Paint, sculpt, draw.
Write a song. Bake a pie.
Keep a journal.

8 CELEBRATE LIFE
Eat good food.
Have a party.
Travel somewhere new.
Laugh a lot.

The Eight Things

Once I returned to life as usual, my priorities were forever shifted. I felt precariously balanced on a precipice, where anything could happen at any time. I learned first-hand that life is precious, and one must focus on making every moment count. Some dormant inner force was awakened, giving me the strength to face my new circumstances as a single woman with renewed hope. There were times I felt lost, but by trial and error, I found my way.

The symbolic significance of having lost the rights to my name was now compounded by the loss of my spouse. Here I was faced with another blank slate and a world of possibilities to explore. Luckily, I had worked hard the past few years to develop a practice aimed at reclaiming my Self.

It's ironic that, just as I was coming to terms with my life after SIGRID OLSEN, I began the long process of taking back control of my name. Curtis' death gave me the impetus I needed to approach the CEO of Liz Claiborne to initiate reclaiming my name. I had lost so much that I felt justified asking for something back from the universe.

As it turned out, after much legal maneuvering we came to an agreement and, nine months later, I had free usage of all my trademarks. This gave me a sense of justice as well as personal triumph, but it also gave my life-long compulsive nature a renewed chance to threaten my equanimity. I was determined to integrate career and my personal life in a way I had never done before, because I was no longer willing to sacrifice my physical and mental health for my work. Creativity and wellness would have to become the **focus**.

What to do now? My journey had taken a turn and I knew in my heart I had to go with it. What worked before was not the answer. This time, I sensed my inherent need for balance would require I use my intuition as a guide. If I resisted the flow (which I tend to do), everything would just be harder.

It all came down to this: the theme of my entire life was built around a core conflict—the inner battle between "letting things happen" and "making them happen." It's the yin and the yang of my personality, this push/pull dynamic.

How do you have the courage to take action, yet allow the river to flow, even if you're uncertain if you can navigate the water? It's like surfing, skiing or stand-up paddle boarding, where you have to embrace the forces of nature to be rewarded with a wonderful ride. I've never been all that good at any of those sports, but fortunately I found yoga. It's become my way to find balance, even amid chaos.

Yoga is all about opposing energies—feet deeply rooted on the earth, with crown chakra reaching towards the sky. No pose is static. There are internal mechanisms at work in everything, and once you become aware of this, it deepens the practice immensely. Each of us finds the balance in our own body. We must push ourselves to move, to take action, but then use gravity, breath and intention to let it all go.

As powerful as the poses are, yoga off the mat is the real teaching. It's like graduate school. My instincts told me that all the internal work I was doing would lead me somewhere better. I was gaining the tools needed to navigate life, even when it was difficult, confusing and disappointing. I could ride the highs and lows yet stay steady on my course. The "doer" in me likes to toss a problem around in my head endlessly, but guess what? It never gets solved by over-thinking. My mind literally drives me crazy.

If only I could silence the noisy thoughts and worries cluttering my mind, then I'd be able to locate that trustworthy inner voice—the one that isn't influenced by ego, intent on pleasing others, or distorted by fear. Then maybe I wouldn't feel so anxious. It's only through my spiritual practice that I'm able to quiet my insanely busy mind and have access to a deeper knowing. If I were my own doctor, I would prescribe strong doses of quiet introversion and meditation, which is one of the many reasons I practice yoga regularly.

The process of finding balance is never-ending. If life were without obstacles and challenges, we wouldn't grow. When I feel out of whack, I have options that will lift me out of the struggle. It doesn't mean I always pay attention. Every moment is a choice and sometimes I disappoint myself by willfully staying in the mixed-up soup of my mind's chatter. I know how to get past it—take a walk on the beach, breathe, meditate, spend time on my mat...but I choose not to, convinced it won't make any difference. And, as is my habit, I tell myself I have too much work to do.

But it's comforting to know that there are practical steps I can take to regain my balance and help evaporate the dark cloud weighing me down. One day, in a flash of insight, I began to write in my journal, organizing the action items into a list of eight things I can always rely on to help me whenever I feel lost—whether it's a heartbreaking event or just a shitty day filled with dark thoughts.

As I wrote, the sequence blossomed so effortlessly that it made everything fall into place.

These eight steps have helped me through many life-changing moments, some huge, others less monumental but still unsettling. If I truly feel off-kilter, I look to this list and, without exception, I can always point to at least a couple of these key components that I've neglected.

When asked how I have overcome the hard times and obstacles in my life inevitably my answer is, "I do the eight things." They are:

1. Connect to nature.
2. Inhabit your body.
3. Find a community.
4. Streamline and simplify.
5. Quiet down.
6. Open your heart.
7. Create.
8. Celebrate life.

1. CONNECT TO NATURE

When my world is clouded with worry, regret or negative thoughts, this is probably the most important and the most instantly effective thing I do. We are not all lucky as I am to live within minutes of a beautiful beach, but we can find smaller doses of nature anywhere—a vase of flowers, an open sky, a flock of birds flying south. Believe it or not, as much as I revere nature, I sometimes get so caught up in work, I have to force myself outdoors into the wild beauty of it.

I have chosen to live in a climate that is gentle most of the time. The mild weather makes it easy to get outside and let nature heal.

During hurricane season each year, however, I'm reminded that everything is tenuous, and easily lost, so I'd better appreciate what I have.

Recently, after Irma almost wiped out my corner of the world, and Maria took its tragic toll in Puerto Rico, I've been searching for peace. With outrageous violence erupting all over the world, daily political disappointments, and a nearly constant barrage of bad news, I have needed to let myself rest in the embrace of nature as a balm for my weary soul. I look around and, inevitably, loveliness appears.

The natural vignettes may be small, but they are there—a sheaf of grasses swaying in the wind, a pulsating gray storm cloud or the sound of birds, like tiny wind instruments in an orchestra—these things give me solace. They make my heart happy, and I am grateful. Sometimes, I even say *thank you*. My need is so great, and the effect is potent, like medicine.

2. INHABIT YOUR BODY

This vessel of mine—I carry it around with me everywhere, but sometimes I'm completely disconnected from it. I let it get stressed, exhausted, over-fed, over-caffeinated, generally over-looked. It's far too easy to disassociate from our bodies. Life gets hectic. We have deadlines to meet, or people to accommodate. And the last thing we take time to do is tune into ourselves. But if we don't listen to our body when it whispers, then eventually it will shout—with disease, depletion, anxiety or depression. I try to nip the dysfunction in the bud.

The first step is to truly feel the effects of stress and stagnation, and then to simply start moving. It doesn't take much. I know every time I choose well—take a lunchtime bike ride, a morning walk on the beach, or an in-depth yoga class—I feel rejuvenated, and I am so glad I did it. Sometimes, because I mostly work at home, I can spontaneously stop and drop in the middle of my day and take ten minutes to stretch out my back on the floor. A few moments in child's pose, a spinal twist and some deep breathing, and I'm good to go.

Speaking of breathing—this is the most basic and overlooked way to inhabit our bodies. If we breathe with our whole being, oxygen will find all those tired, achy, captive corners of ourselves that need to be released. The yogic breathing technique of pranayama, literally brings energy (prana) to every cell of our bodies.

There are many ways to awaken the physical self; it doesn't have to be yoga. Dancing is wonderful, as is running, skating, snowboarding, biking or even making love.

I happen to enjoy activities that combine more than one of the healing steps, especially if they involve productivity, like gardening—where I'm out in nature, bending, moving and lifting things—engrossed in beauty and enabling plants to flourish. The feel of the soil and rich aroma of plant life sustains the better parts of me. And, in the end, I get to enjoy the fruits of my labor. To be creative, enjoy nature, and use my body while in a lovely setting—this is the best medicine I've found.

Even walking does the trick. The rhythmic action is like a mantra—Thich Nhat Hanh calls it "walking meditation". For example, if I feel anger and frustration boiling up inside, I go for a walk. I pace furiously along the water's edge, concentrating on the ebb and flow of the surf, while I repeat some (possibly expletive-ridden) phrase in my head, over and over, until I don't feel angry anymore and the words have lost all their power. I take negative thoughts and apply positive action.

Another aspect of inhabiting one's body is to feed it well. The subject of healthy eating would fill volumes, so I'm not going to attempt to address it here. It's no secret that food and wellness are intrinsically interconnected. When I nourish myself well, I feel better. I eat lightly, and my outlook is more buoyant. Prolonged over-indulgence definitely slows me down, makes it harder for me to access my happiness. When I focus on how I want to **feel**, rather than how I want to **look**, it is so much easier for me to make healthy choices.

Aging is an additional challenge when it comes to loving and nurturing our physical selves. I didn't appreciate how much things change, especially for women, after menopause, until I experienced it myself. Realistically, no amount of exercise or organic produce can stop the wrinkles, the sagging skin, the mood swings, the aches and occasional fatigue from over-exertion, but it can definitely help. So does self-acceptance. It's okay not to be perfect.

After a certain age, I don't care to compete. I don't need my breasts to defy gravity, or my face to be unlined and static. The scars I've collected each tell a story that is part of my life's narrative. I am proud to have survived. I'm grateful for my strength and flexibility and work hard to maintain it. I can always work harder, but I'd rather relax and have fun, so I've learned to accept myself as I am.

My father, by example, taught me never to quit moving. A native New Yorker, much of his life he lived in walk-up apartments, usually on the fourth or fifth floor. He never just walked up, but usually sprinted, sometimes taking two steps at a time, good-naturedly shaming me if I was slow. Even in his advanced years, he imagined himself a younger man, doing as much as he could, even when his body refused to cooperate. He was devoted to his daily swim at the Y into his early nineties, joking that it took him a half hour to get there, another half hour to get undressed, for a fifteen-minute circuit in the pool, followed by another hour of showering, changing and getting back home, whether by taxi, or chauffeured by his (only slightly) younger wife. His body simply gave out seven months before his ninety-ninth birthday, but his spirit, dimmed by age, remained strong.

3. FIND A COMMUNITY

We are all interconnected. We need each other. It takes clear intention to reach out and build valuable connections and create a deep sense of community. Choose people who support and love the best in you. People who inspire and are inspired by you. People who are truly present. What about family? You don't choose them, but you have the choice to be clean, clear and unmessy in your relationships. Remove the obstacles to communication—judgment, worry, guilt, fear, anger, resentment. Let go of these and watch what happens.

I admit there is nothing worse than feeling completely alone. I believe isolation is at the core of our pernicious societal malaise; even acts of terrorism are often attributed to the loner who wants to belong to something greater. All of this is exacerbated by the massive amount of time and energy we spend on our electronic devices. While I am a fan of social media (I feel it helps me stay connected and is a way to reflect my full persona), it's not the real thing. No matter what we are going through—pain, loss, suffering—it's made easier when there is someone to listen, to look into our eyes, and to hold on to, if that's what is needed. Extra points if they make you laugh.

Every time I've hit a wall, suffered a loss, or felt hopeless, there's been someone there to lift me up. It doesn't take much to be someone's support. We talk in yoga about "holding space" for others. What does this mean? For me, it's about **being**, not **doing**. You show up, with an open mind, a compassionate heart and you just…wait. Create a sense of safety for one another, give wild emotions time to settle and let the space around you be filled with an unspoken gesture of love. Words sometimes take time to come.

When Curtis died, I really felt the power of community. All of a sudden, an invisible safety net appeared, and I was lifted up on a cloud of love and support from every direction. I felt protected by an enormous circle of positive energy. I knew that whatever I needed would be provided. It's at times like these when you realize that every bit of generosity you ever showed to anyone comes back a thousand-fold.

Women have a particular talent for creating community. We long for sisterly connection, especially when life gets complicated. As we learn the basics of how to interact selflessly (showing kindness, withholding criticism, releasing guilt, worry, anger and resentment), we begin to put our truest, most authentic self forward. We create a safe space, and then are more able to share the tough stuff, the shitty feelings, and the toxic thoughts, without fear of judgment.

I see the virtue of this interaction every day on my retreats. In just eight years, our informal community has already crystallized into a beautiful extended family. Something remarkable has happened. Women from all over the country, with various backgrounds, of different ages and circumstances come together for a similar purpose—to claim a moment for ourselves. Recognizing the need for rest, replenishment and introspection, we commit to a week of self-care by joining one another on retreat. What we've discovered about ourselves has created a bond that endures over time and distance. Rarely do I see such a powerful example of community as this.

We get to define family any way we want. As a child of the sixties, I've always leaned towards a communal existence. I'm still a fan of the collective consciousness, which epitomized that era. As an art student, and into my twenties, my friends and I lived in various communal assemblages of our self-created tribe. It was unstructured, heart-felt, and always interesting. We believed life would always be like that.

Of course, things have changed. Somehow, through all the rigors of the day-to-day, the unexpected shit-storms, and general life challenges, I still have an innate love and respect for most humans and I enjoy finding common ground. Wherever I am, I'm drawn to finding or creating community.

Almost always, it gives me joy to raise someone else's spirits. There was a time, just a few years ago, after my husband's sudden passing, when I opened my home and heart to three young women friends. We called it the **ashram**. By definition, **ashram** is a Hindu term describing a religious retreat or monastic community. In our looser sense of the word, it was a place of refuge for kindred spirits in need of safety during transition. Their companionship helped turn a potentially difficult period for me into one of my happiest memories.

I'd just made the brave solo move to a big canal-front house on Siesta Key from the ease of condo living in Downtown Sarasota. I'd been warned against it, especially now in my new widowed state.

"It's too much work to maintain a house, especially as a single woman. Wouldn't you rather be able to turn the key when you walk out the door and never have to worry?"

Actually, no. I desperately wanted to be able to step out my door onto the earth, without the use of an elevator. I wanted to plant a garden, listen to birds in the morning, and have space to spread out and create art. I'd enjoyed the lovely bay-front condo that Curtis and I shared as a first home in Florida, but I was ready to move on. I needed a complete change.

Moving into the big bungalow-style home on Siesta Key was a huge first for me. I'd moved plenty of times, but always with a husband, or kids—now I was alone in this rental, making decisions, arranging the furniture, and setting the tone. I fell deeply in love with the house, like you do with a new lover. I literally never wanted to leave. It gave me such a sense of peaceful domesticity. But it was lonely.

The depth of my loneliness surprised me. It brought me right back to the sadness of my childhood. I gave myself permission to explore that feeling…to sit with it until I understood that my longing for connection wasn't something to be ashamed of, but simply part of being human.

Once I got settled, I realized I wanted to share the beauty of this place with other people. So, one by one, I invited these sweet friends to come and take a breather at my house, while they figured out what was next. It may have seemed generous, but to be honest, it was as much for me as it was for them.

Our lives had intersected in different ways, but now they were each temporarily displaced and needed not just shelter, but a safe place with a positive vibe to sort things out. For a few extraordinary months, the four of us cohabited easily, coming and going freely, and sharing our own personal stories of heartbreak, redemption and self-discovery. The **ashram** was imbued with a gentle, vibrant energy that transformed and sustained us while we sorted things out. We ate lovely meals, drank wine, practiced yoga, had parties, made art, wrote beautiful poetry, sang karaoke and talked late into the night under a canopy of stars.

One particular night when we were all together, I suddenly realized, with crystal clear insight, that this was a brief moment in time. The evening was dense with tropical humidity, as we settled out on the deck for a glass of wine and a little conversation—our usual gathering spot. I looked at each of their unique and beautiful faces, knowing the pain they had endured and reflected on the incredible growth we'd gained, living together under this roof. With a mixture of sadness and foresight, I said:

"Stop and remember this moment. It won't last forever...it's just a snapshot in time. The image will fade, but we will always remember how special it was."

And we have. Eventually we all went our separate ways. It was as though all we needed was a short window to regroup, and then we were ready to meet life's challenges with renewed passion and determination. The four of us are still a galvanized unit—we stay in touch and feel connected, even as we follow our independent paths. Like this, we can all continue to weave the tapestry of criss-crossed threads that will enrich our lives.

4. STREAMLINE AND SIMPLIFY

When life gets tricky and tangled, I yearn for something plain and simple. Clean. Natural. Open space—quiet and expansive with room to breathe.

We spend so much of our lives flirting with complexity, accumulating things. It's actually easier than you think to just let it go. There's a feeling of lightness and freedom that comes with detachment from material objects. After sifting through drawers and closets, organizing and weeding out unnecessary items, I feel I've taken positive action. Often, it's the only way to feel I have power over something in my life.

Streamlining my surroundings is a potent antidote to stress. (Perhaps it's just another avoidance mechanism?) But when my heart is heavy, or my mind is clouded with troubling thoughts, you can usually find me somewhere in the house, **folding**. Anything— towels, laundry, the basket of cashmere wraps I keep near the door. I call it "anxiety folding", and it's especially helpful when I am pissed off and trying not to be.

To some degree, we are all affected by our surroundings and are better off without clutter. In my workspace, I feel uneasy if things get too chaotic. I'm one of those creative souls who needs a clean surface to initiate a project, but once I'm in the zone, it could be days before I tidy up. When I'm fully engaged, I can live for quite a while with mild chaos occupying my table, floor, desk, or all of the above. I see it as the natural ebb and flow of the creative process, and it doesn't bother me much. Unless I'm in a psychological tizzy, and then it just adds to my despair.

When my company closed in 2008, it was definitely a signal to re-examine my priorities. I had spent the last couple of decades growing the business, adding to my personal stash of houses, furniture, clothes, shoes, and other goodies, climbing a ladder with no end in sight. Now it was time to sell the big house, clean out my closets, and reverse the tide from collecting to discarding.

Once I wrapped my head around that, I was eager to get started. The upheaval gave us the opportunity to make life simple again. Clearly, we needed to limit our outflow of expenses and learn to conserve. It would be a relief to let go of all the excess and have a fresh start. Why fight it? The old chapter was over; I was already onto the next one.

Four yard sales later, we successfully downsized to enable us to live in our one-bedroom cottage, and it felt wonderful. Since that time, I've collected and discarded numerous times, but ultimately it's the letting go that makes me happiest. Once you experience the Zen concept of less is more, it's very alluring.

Simplifying is not just about cleaning out closets and getting rid of excess stuff. Also, we have to take a hard look at the thoughts, people, and habits that drain our energy and complicate everything unnecessarily. It takes emotional courage, unwavering honesty and stark clarity see the patterns of behavior that we allow to disrupt our personal equilibrium. For many of us, we say yes when, for our own peace of mind, it might be more honest to say no. We take on more than we should, and then feel overwhelmed.

I know I do. When I am feeling really healthy and centered, I know how to safeguard my psyche from the drama of others, while still showing compassion and love. But when I'm not vigilant, my "superstar" Ms. Fixit persona accepts more and more responsibility, disruption, and stress, until I can't take it anymore. Then I need to wipe the slate clean (thank you, nature, yoga, meditation, laughter with friends) to refresh my soul, so I can go about the business of being human without depleting my reserves.

Big lesson here: what happens when you make more space? Something always comes in to fill the void. Wonderful unexpected things. But if you never clear out the old energy, there's no way for the new energy to refresh your life.

I've found that as I slowly disentangle from complexity, I have more time to enjoy and appreciate what I do have, what I have chosen to keep. A cleaner environment allows beauty to be noticed. Small things become important There are more quiet moments to let my thoughts expand into. The same holds true for the more difficult releases- that of toxic relationships, unhealthy decisions and counter-intuitive actions.

There is a Sanskrit term, *santosha*, which means acceptance, being OK with what is. That path seems impossible at times. But once I set my intention in that direction, a space opens up and my personal energy current is revitalized with a positive flow.

5. QUIET DOWN

The world is a noisy place. Perhaps we live in a city—with constant traffic and streets bloated with people, horns, sirens— providing incessant cacophony. Maybe we keep the TV or radio on all day "for company" or find ourselves bombarded with newsfeed, social media, online notifications, bells, dings, rings and buzzers. Sometimes, it's all just too much.

Even without external annoyances, our minds can overflow with too much internal chatter. That's when it's time to check out. Escape all the commotion and simply **be**. Easier said than done, I know. Usually, it takes a change of location (move to a quiet room or, better yet, and outdoor sanctuary like a grassy field or stretch of sandy beach.) When I'm in the city, and none of the natural cures are available, that's when I slip into a yoga studio for a little replenishment. At the end of every session, no matter how strenuous, there's always a blissful rest period called *savasana* where the entire class lies still, drifting into an altered state of inner quiet and complete rest. I can literally feel my cells rejuvenate from the brief interval of supine silence.

A favorite meme of mine, attributed to author, Anne Lamott:

"Almost anything will work again if you unplug it for a few minutes. Even you."

As healing as quiet time can be, solitude and silence can be frightening for some. In our society, we are accustomed to being

~ 263 ~

surrounded with people, even if we don't want to be. Sometimes, we even choose unpleasant company over being alone. Solitude is scary. There is an emptiness that feels like it will never be filled. I've learned, as a survivor of childhood loneliness, one can learn how to be OK alone. Quiet solitude helps me connect to the moment without distraction. I feel more present and, even if my mind is overly full, eventually I tune into a sense of peace I didn't even realize was there. The older I get, the more I value the peace of **not doing.**

6. OPEN YOUR HEART

I am, by nature, a generous person. The well-being and happiness of those I love (and even those I know peripherally) is important to me. I have a deep belief that the more you give, the more you get, though that is not necessarily what motivates me. Quite simply, it makes me happy to bring other people joy, even in a small way. The best is when I can provide the intangible—advice, support, love, humor, compassion—to help make this tricky business of living just a little better.

Often, we have no idea what impact even the smallest of gestures has on other people. It takes so little to boost someone's morale, to encourage him or her to keep at it when the going gets tough. Usually, the hidden reward in this type of consideration is the undeniable lift it gives our own spirit to see we have made a difference in someone else's life.

Like most people, I have days when I can't seem to penetrate the dark cloud surrounding me. The weight of my anxiety, regret, worry, or fear encases me like a straightjacket, and I'm unable to break through. I feel on the verge of tears, or wake up panicked in the night, for no obvious reason, just gripped by a vague despair. I know that light and love are on the other side of this, within reach, but I resign myself to the momentary gloom, hoping it will pass by tomorrow.

I had a day like this recently on a work trip in New York City. I was feeling a tad hopeless (granted, more than a few of the **eight things** had been ignored) walking aimlessly around the city. I had some time to kill between my workday and meeting my daughter for dinner in Soho. It was rush hour and I braved the crowded subway to head downtown. My mind was so jammed with thoughts; it felt like rush hour in my brain. I needed something, unsure what (probably a good twenty minutes of mindful meditation), but instead, I somehow ended up lost in Chinatown.

The darkening night reminded me of my first trips to Hong Kong, where I spent endless hours alone, wandering streets that looked just like this. A barrage of sounds—street vendors, tinkly music, car horns, fire engines—added to my edginess. I couldn't seem to shake it.

In the midst of all the craziness, I spotted a simple, Zen-like teahouse and gravitated toward it, as if magnetized by the calm environment inside. As I juggled the multiple bags I was carrying to access the correct eyewear to read the tea menu, I was approached by a pretty young Chinese girl seated at a nearby table.

"Can I please ask you just one question?" she murmured shyly. I turned to see her, hard at work on her laptop, and something in me sensed that just a few words from me might help her with whatever challenge she was up against. "Why not? I have time now," I thought to myself.

"Sure. What is it?"

"Well, I'm not sure how to fill out this job application. Can you please take a look? It says here to fill in the position I am applying for, but do I add in the company name too?"

"Let me take a look, I am not sure I understand." I am such a visual person; I had to see it in black and white to be fully informed. So, I reviewed her application and then asked her a few questions about herself. She had just graduated from F.I.T. (aha—a fashion student!) and was doing an online job search. I asked if I could see her resume and the list of positions she was considering. I told her that I was actually in the fashion business myself and had been for over thirty years.

"Really? That's amazing! Thank you so much!"

I began to review her online documents, leaning over to see the laptop screen, still holding all my bags and coat, since it was overly warm inside.

"May I sit down? I think it would be easier."

"Of course, thank you. I am so grateful to have you help me!"

She was so sweet and appreciative, but I had done nothing, really. I just gave her my full attention for a brief time and that made all the difference. We looked over all the job postings and I helped her recognize which were the most aligned with her skills and advised her where to direct her search. We talked for about twenty minutes, and then we connected on LinkedIn. She clicked on my profile and looked at me with wide eyes, clearly impressed.

"You are CEO? Wow. Thanks so much for taking time with me."

I had to laugh inwardly because my title sounded much more grand than it was. At this point, I alone comprised the entire staff I governed. Granted, I'd had a long history as an accomplished designer and executive, but those days were in the rearview mirror.

I don't know how much impact that chance meeting had on my new young friend, but I left the tea house (never having had a chance to order a cup) feeling as if a weight had been lifted. The dark cloud was gone, and I felt happy to be of use.

This is just a small example of how giving of one's self delivers benefits far beyond what we've given.

Generosity breeds abundance. Selfishness only creates scarcity and isolation. Often, the simple act of being fully present is the greatest gift to another person.

I am always moved to do something bigger, more dramatic to help humanity, yet haven't found the courage or the opportunity to step into a truly dangerous or desperate situation. But I haven't ruled it out either. I know if and when the circumstance appears, I will be the one who will be remarkably changed. That's the gift that keeps on giving.

7. CREATE

I believe we are all inherently creative. It manifests in various ways, but the simple act of making something out of nothing is like a miracle, whether it's a sculpture, a flower arrangement, a melody strummed on the guitar, a birthday cake, a poem or a painting. This ability to design, devise and create is one of the true gifts of being human.

Children take such pleasure in their artwork, which they do freely, without inhibition. Sadly, at some point in life, our inner artist is squelched by other forces—conformity, criticism, the judgmental voices of others. The goal of the art workshops I lead on retreat is to help people silence their internal critics (we have only one rule: no shit-talking your own work) and learn to have fun again, making stuff together.

The more I ponder the creative process, I realize how essential it is to life. For me, it's like breathing. Not just because it comes naturally, but also because it requires IN and OUT - inhale inspiration and exhale creation.

I can't go too long taking in beauty without wanting to give it life. I love visiting museums, galleries, seeing street art and fashion shows, but before long, I have an overwhelming desire to put that inspiration into work—on paper, with fabric, or even on the table for dinner.

I know my soul feels depleted when creativity is absent from my life. It was my crutch as an only child. Filling long, lonely hours with color and pattern kept me amused and engaged.

I learned a few important things in art school, and not just about art. There are design principles that also apply to life:

- Less is more.
- Dive in. Think later.
- Form follows function.
- Don't overwork it.
- All is possible. Life is a blank canvas every day.

Creativity is the fuel that has driven me all my life. Fortunately, I found my way to a career that could hold all my ideas. I built a business that was infinitely receptive to every inspiration I had with no end to the number of products that needed an injection of my color, print and artistic expertise. In fact, it was so expansive that I couldn't do it alone. I gathered a team of designers who were motivated in the very same way, not by money or fame, but by the pure joy of seeing concepts come to life. It was a wonderful gift to share that energy with them.

But then, after the corporate merger, with each added executive responsibility, my position as Creative Director became exponentially less creative. Eventually, I managed the people who managed the people who did the creative work. I attended countless meetings to decide what we would create and how it would be sold. During the last years of my reign at SIGRID OLSEN, I barely touched a pencil or a paintbrush at all. I kept thinking I would get to it when I finished my urgent to-do list, but I never did.

When the company closed, and the daily tasks were erased from my calendar, I had nothing but time on my hands. It took me a while to embrace this monumental change, but once I did, I hungrily devoured every opportunity to apply my color sense and use my hands again.

The first thing I did was to go out and by a Mac laptop and learn to use it. I'd never considered myself to be very computer savvy, but this new machine felt like just another tool in my art kit. I fell in love with it as a new medium. Once I grasped the basics, I taught myself how to design my own website, which provided a focus for my creative energy.

I was building a business again, but this time it was tiny, human-scaled, and none of it required corporate approval. I absorbed every aspect of the new venture and poured my heart into it. It was minuscule compared to my previous enterprise, but the advantage was this: I could do it all by myself. Whatever idea came into my head, I could make it happen. No meetings. No power point presentation. No focus group or viability study. I could just **do it**... That realization made my heart soar. I woke up every morning revved up and ready to get to work.

The beauty of this new job I gave myself was that every day was different. Some days, I would do research, get inspiration, or take photos for my website. I had no predetermined schedule, but I was working all the time, though it felt more like play, to be honest. Prohibited contractually from designing clothes, I was forced to direct my energy elsewhere.

Naturally, my first instinct was to pick up painting again, after having abandoned it once I returned to work, after my breast surgery, three years prior. That brief time off gave me a small window to germinate the seed of an idea, but it was only a month—not long enough for it to fully bloom. When my break was finished, and I returned to work, I became fully consumed by the job again. It took another major catastrophe to take me back full circle to my roots as an artist. Now, I had all the time in the world. I'd seen the healing effect of creativity after my medical leave, and was instinctively drawn to it again.

I designed my new website to promote the sale of paintings instead of fashion, using the mailing list provided by my customer service department at Liz. Once I reached out to my customers and told a bit of my story, via a newly designed blog, I was rewarded by the enthusiastic support of women who had wondered what happened to me after all my stores had closed. I reconnected, and it felt amazing. Several of these cyber-clients responded by ordering custom artwork, and I got to painting again.

Funny, how I needed orders to spur my productivity. A designer at heart, I was wired for commerce. The impetus of their specific requests inspired the artwork I was about to produce. For instance, one piece included poetry my customer's daughter had written, and another sent me the color of her wall as context for the tropical scene she wanted in her newly redecorated bedroom. The personal requirements of these commissions could have felt restrictive, but it gave me direction. It was actually heartwarming to uplift people's spirits in this way.

This has become my mantra in everything I do—bring beauty into people's lives and create positive vibes. Being able to touch another's heart with my art is the ultimate gift, and it gives me a sense of purpose, which I desperately needed then and still do today.

One Christmas season, I went through a period where I hand-painted dozens of sheets of paper and used them for wrapping presents. Watercolor washes and stripes were over-printed with my hand-carved stamps. I worked feverishly, repeating the motion with wide brushes, over-and-over with a full array of colors for hours on end. When Curtis came into my studio one day and saw the entire floor littered with sheets of multi-hues pages and my table a riot of color, he asked me what I was doing.

"I have no idea. I just started painting and now I can't stop!"

That's the kind of creative energy that has a life of its own. Loose, free, effortless and exciting. It's the nirvana that I'm always seeking, but rarely achieve. When I've gone too long without it, I miss it.

Then…I discovered ceramics. Asked by an old friend, who is a master potter, to paint a small bowl for a Food Pantry benefit, I had my first taste of applying my art in three dimensions. I quickly painted a few bowls and was ravenous for more. She showed me that I could order anything I wanted online—white bisque ware in all shapes and sizes—and all I had to do was apply colored glazes and have them fired. I went crazy. Soon huge boxes came to my door filled with bare bowls, plates, mugs and serving platters, which I accepted gratefully. I bought pints of colored glazes, brushes and sgraffito tools and was soon immersed in a whole new medium for my work. I developed a technique where I painted my signature motifs (birds, fish, starfish, shells, leaves, flowers) in beautiful colors and inscribed them with a sharply pointed sgraffito tool, to give added dimension.

It felt wonderful to be making something with my hands again—objects that people would buy and use. In a small way, my pieces would become a part of their lives. Hand-painted ceramics soon became the bestsellers in my gallery. I have painted and sold hundreds of pieces over the past decade. The more I made, the more I sold, and it buoyed my spirits to have this new outlet for my creativity. I was compelled to keep my hand in the game while I figured out the next big thing.

Though manual labor is time consuming, if it's satisfying creatively, then the time is well-spent. I recall thinking to myself as I looked at the tabletop full of bowls and platters I'd just painted, "I spent four hours painting pottery and look at this. In my old job, I would have wasted the same four hours in a meeting with nothing to show when we were done."

Thus became my life. I could retrieve a kiln-load of ceramics from the folks who fired for me, bring it home, display in my gallery, photograph each piece, upload the shots to my computer to select for my website, all in one day. The paintings I created in my studio were framed and hung within hours of completion. The artwork was also scanned and made into greeting cards, which we printed and packaged right there on site. Every weekend and during summer months, customers visited the art colony where my home/gallery was located and viewed my work, commented and even bought it. The cycle from concept to sale was shortened far beyond anything I had every designed in all my years in fashion. Instant creative gratification was my new drug of choice.

The gallery became my portal to the outside world. Soon, we opened a small clothing boutique nearby and another one in Florida a few years later. My creative energy was fully utilized, but I knew that this was probably unsustainable. Eventually, I would have to expand beyond my small footprint and find a larger outlet for my work to make a living.

My instincts were correct. Once I re-entered the world of fashion in 2014, especially now without the help of my husband, something had to give. I decided to close my retail galleries and boutiques and focus on gainful work I could do at home, without forfeiting my retreats, which have become the embodiment of my most cherished work.

This course of action has brought me so much happiness, and creative wellbeing continues to draw me with a mysterious pull. There is something about facilitating the act of creation in a beautiful setting with willing participants that feels like my calling. It's amazing to watch other people get lost in the creative process. I know from experience how alluring it can be, but to witness this type of renewal in others, time-and-time again, is truly fulfilling.

I see it happen on almost every retreat or art workshop I lead. There are always one or two people who skip lunch, forget the time, or have to be dragged out of the art room to move on to the next activity. The rest of us have gone about our day and, hours later, come back to find a guest or two bent over the worktable, surrounded by paper, ink pads and hand-carved stamps, unable to pull themselves away. The magnetism of making art is just too strong.

~ 273 ~

8. CELEBRATE LIFE

In a way, this step outshines all the other seven. Far too often, we forget to have fun. Days, even weeks, go by and we haven't gathered with friends, laughed out loud, or set the table for more than one or two. Maybe we feel undeserving, guilty for some reason, or just too busy with more serious matters. But there is nothing that quite equals the feeling of pure joy that comes from a good party.

No matter how treacherous or unforgiving life can be, I try to find cause for celebration. When life feels like a tough slog, or simply a mindless routine, I look at the situation and ask: "Is there joy to be had?" If not, it needs fixing.

Not too long ago, I was searching for a new way to express the essence of my clothing line in my advertising images. We have always been about happiness and uplifting messages, but it occurred to me that maybe I hadn't taken that far enough.

Fashion has a sub-text that makes me uncomfortable. It's one thing to show the glitzy, polished styles that we all admire, but there is a dark side to this aspirational imagery that often causes insecurity and anxiety in women and young girls. We aren't cool enough, thin enough, pretty enough or can't afford the latest trends. I wanted to break that mold and show happy people, having a good time together, feeling comfortable, and looking beautiful, wearing my designs. **For real**.

In the old days, we devoted an enormous part of our budget to photo shoots and media buys. The pictures were gorgeous and impressive, and they achieved the objective we set for the brand...to establish Sigrid Olsen in the forefront of our industry, with the inherent promise that the clothes would make the wearer stylish, happy and well-dressed. Nowadays my company operates on a more personal scale and reflects my own lifestyle more closely.

This point was driven home when we decided that I, at age 64, would step into the role, not just as designer, but also as model for my own wares. The message is this: Aging doesn't have to be a downer. It was fun (as well as cost-saving!), and I marveled at the fact that now, in my sixties, I was more comfortable in front of the camera than during my "peak years," in my twenties and thirties. However, pictures of me, in professional hair and makeup, posing for the camera, didn't really tell the whole story. I wanted it to reflect the real me, enjoying the very best part of life...how we celebrate.

The practical reality of our tiny budget was a determining factor as well. It no longer made fiscal sense to spend thousands of dollars on a shoot when the photos were to be featured on my website and social media, instead of on the pages of Vogue or Harper's Bazaar. The financial challenge actually spurred me to reimagine how I could present my brand to the world in a new way.

The truth is, my chosen lifestyle not only uplifts my spirits, but inspires others as well. My goal as a retreat leader and even as a designer is to show women how to access joy in their lives, and I envisioned my next photo shoot as an attempt to communicate that. It was time to merge both sides of my life—creative wellbeing and business.

I thought: Why not just do what I naturally love to do?

So, in 2017, almost ten years after the close of my company, I launched a campaign that captured my real passion: celebrating life with people I love. I invited a group of my closest female friends to my house for an alfresco dinner in our back yard. To set the tone, we carefully prepared the table outdoors, overlooking the canal, with twinkly lights encircling the patio, and set the table with yards of my original print fabric and colorful flowers. I created a signature cucumber martini cocktail and shared the recipe on my website. My foodie friends brought beautiful platters of stunning vegetables and mouth-watering cheeses.

I gave each guest her choice of clothing to wear, and we all settled in for an evening of camaraderie and fun. Instead of hiring a fashion photographer with a crew and mounds of equipment, I located an event photographer who specialized in capturing "the good life". It was a big success. The photos captured the lighthearted spontaneity of females gathering to enjoy a gorgeous evening, eat fabulous food and share stories together. Some had never met, others were old friends, but by the end of the night it didn't matter. We were all swept up in the celebration, and the photos came out just as I had pictured—a visual confirmation of the fact that, it's not just about the clothes, but something deeper, even euphoric, that resonates with women everywhere.

The message was clear:

Life is to be celebrated every chance you get.

About Sigrid Olsen

Sigrid is an artist, fashion designer and entrepreneur with over 30 years of experience in the apparel industry. Her company grew from a small, home-based business in 1984 to an internationally acclaimed fashion brand with a presence in most major department stores, specialty stores and over fifty SIGRID OLSEN boutiques across the U.S. and Canada. Her company was acquired in 1999 by apparel giant Liz Claiborne Inc. where the business enjoyed several years of phenomenal growth until it was discontinued in 2008.

Since that time, Sigrid has emerged as a lifestyle-driven thought leader, with a focus on creative wellbeing. In 2009, she established her unique art & yoga infused *Inspiration Retreats*, and she has personally hosted dozens of small groups of women in locales around the world, including Tulum, Mexico, Tuscany, Provence, California and Florida.

Sigrid's story has been featured in many major publications including the New York Times, Women's Wear Daily, Wall Street Journal, O The Oprah Magazine, More Magazine, Boston Globe, Sarasota Magazine, and Coastal Living Magazine, as well as on radio and television.

As a designer with an enduring customer base, Sigrid has inspired her audience through a relaxed, upbeat approach to fashion, an inherent love of textile design, and a remarkably close connection to her consumer. Today, Sigrid's company has evolved into SIGRID OLSEN: New Designs for Living. This umbrella encompasses all aspects of design, as well as a personal lifestyle focus on health and happiness that resonates with women everywhere.

Sigrid resides and works out of her home studio on Siesta Key in Sarasota, Florida.

Photo Credit: Troy Plota

Books by Sigrid Olsen

SIGRID OLSEN MY LIFE Redesigned: Embracing Change, Aging Gracefully, and Finding Magic in the Simple Things

LIFECRAFT: A Guided Journal for an Inspired Life --- Coming Soon!

NOURISH: A Creative Wellbeing Cookbook --- Coming Soon!

BONUS EXCERPTS

LIFECRAFT

A Guided Journal for an Inspired Life

BY

SIGRID OLSEN

Rediscover Your Inner Artist

& Access Your Authentic Self

Manifesting: one, two, three...

A few years ago, while on retreat in Mexico, I had an epiphany. We had spent the day exploring what it takes to see a dream to fruition and I began to see a pattern. I thought of all the different things I had accomplished over the years, both large and small, and realized that the process of manifestation comes down to three basic steps. By instinct, I've followed this course of action and find that it applies to any ambition, whether tiny or gargantuan.

Step One: Set the Intention

This is harder than it sounds. It's critical to get clarity around what it is you want. We've all fallen victim to "watch out what you wish for" when we use the wrong criteria to set our intention. Journaling is a good method to collect the rush of thoughts and ideas, and then you must edit and check in with your heart to see if it feels right. If your vision aligns with your true nature, it will unfold gracefully. Even so, it helps to be very focused, but also fluid, since sometimes as you progress, the tides will turn, and it will require a change of tack.

Step Two: Do the Work

Yes, work is unavoidable. Too often we hear about the law of attraction, assuming it means that if you think the right thoughts your dream will magically come to you. We assume it will simply manifest if we are aligned with the right energy. The truth is, however, if you align with your goal, the work will drive you. It takes dedication, determination and focus, but if the process is fueled by true passion, then your energy to accomplish it will be limitless. Nothing can be accomplished without sincere work and brutal honesty.

Step Three: Have Faith

What happens when it feels like the work isn't working? Sometimes it seems there are obstacles at every turn. That's when this step is most important. Faith is the same thing as patience. Most of us want immediate results, proof that we are on the right track. Unfortunately, quite often this takes time and we simply have to keep focused, continue working and watch as it all comes together.

I try never to think too far ahead, and try to enjoy the process of creativity, keeping my sights on the future, while allowing for opportunities that I cannot even envision. The challenge of orchestrating the diverse aspects of launching any new endeavor is something I approach without a formal business plan, trying to get clarity, until a clear path reveals itself to me. The thrill of doing it my way, not adhering to a strict protocol feels right. For some, veering away from the mainstream might seem frightening, but for me it is the only way to go.

That's Why They Call It a Practice

So, we have the eight things, and we've learned how to manifest. We cleared out negative energy, re-connected with nature, tapped into creativity, learned to meditate, cleaned up our food act, found our tribe, and even began to have more fun. Now what?

Life is still chaotic and unpredictable.

It takes two seconds of uncertainty/rushing/discord/stress and we are right back where we started, or so it seems. The moment we feel that jangly unsteadiness that comes with the friction of real life, we judge ourselves harshly. We think: "Shit, I haven't changed as much as I thought. I get thrown off so easily. My equilibrium is shaky, my self-esteem is wobbly, I'm a hot mess."

This happens to me so often I can only conclude one thing. It's okay.

We just keep on keeping on. Don't waste time feeling bad about getting off track. Life is too short. There is beauty lingering just beyond the dark, like the sun obstructed by an ominous cloud cover. Even if we do nothing, it will pass. But if we return to the things that we know will heal us, the energy changes more quickly, even if it seems insurmountable at the time.

The simple act of reclaiming one's own soul is a triumph. In our hearts we know what to do, but sometimes we forget. Go ahead— bundle up and take a walk outside, even in the bitter cold, roll out your yoga mat, if only for five minutes, turn off the noise, find a friend who will listen, write in your journal, take the opportunity to meditate no matter where you are. Don't think, just do. Give your dampened spirit a jump-start and it will know what to do.

That's why they call it a practice.

FINDING BALANCE

One of the first exercises I created for my Inspiration retreats was the "Life Balance" chart. The idea came to me one day when I was reflecting on how different I felt in the year after my business closed compared to the years prior when I was under deadlines, working 60+ hour weeks, juggling single motherhood and rushing, rushing, rushing all the time.

What was I doing differently? Where was I spending my time and energy now? I still worked every day, launching my website, networking with various colleagues, establishing my retail gallery and shop.

But I felt healthier, more energized...balanced. Why?

The simple answer was that now I had control of my time and my environment. I hadn't abandoned my nature as an overachiever, but I calibrated my days to suit myself and enhance my wellbeing. I was able to sneak in a yoga class mid-morning and eat my homemade lunch outside in the sun at noon. I could choose who to be with and how we would interact. I had time alone to think and create.

I have come up with six elements that are integral for most of us in our lives. The idea is to track where your energy goes not necessarily the time you spend in each activity. What I discovered after working with many groups of women is that most of us are focused mostly on one or two areas and the rest are on the back burner. Often work or caring for others takes over our lives. Sometimes we are generous to a fault, giving without taking time to replenish our reserves. We might even regard focusing on ourselves as an act of extreme selfishness. But, it is each of our responsibility to care for our SELF. The reward for this is a life that feels balanced, productive, and *happy*.

The six elements:

1. Livelihood
2. Connection
3. Creativity
4. Health
5. Solitude
6. Fun

JOURNAL NOTES:

Take a moment to reflect on the questions posed in each of the above categories. Write a few words or insights that come to mind regarding the importance of each one in your life.

DIVIDING UP YOUR PIE CHART: Once you have given some thought to the above, then you are ready to divide up your pie chart. The one shown is the IDEAL...no one is perfect and has all the elements exactly in balance. Also, things change from time-to-time...so this process can be repeated periodically. The idea is to increase your **awareness** and understanding—that *you* have the power to make choices to enhance (or deplete) your energy.

Please note: When you fill in your own pie chart think about where the majority of your energy is spent...not necessarily time. A job can take up 1/3 to 1/2 of your day, but it can also feed you creatively, provide a sense of purpose and community. Or it can drain you and prevent you from having time to do the things that feed your soul.

How to use the LIFE BALANCE PIE CHART:

LIFE BALANCE PIE CHART

IDEAL LIFE IN BALANCE:

- livelihood
- connection
- creativity
- health
- solitude
- fun

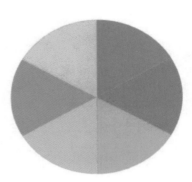

REALITY:

Create a pie chart that
reflects where you are **now**
in terms of your life balance.

*Use this as a tool anytime
you feel the need to
recalibrate your life.*

NOURISH

A Creative Wellbeing Cookbook

Artfully Original Recipes by

SIGRID OLSEN